The First Weeks of
School

Laying a Quality Foundation

The First Weeks of
School

Laying a Quality Foundation

JANE PERLMUTTER & LOUISE BURRELL

HEINEMANN • PORTSMOUTH, NH

Heinemann
A division of Reed Elsevier Inc.
361 Hanover Street
Portsmouth, NH 03801–3912
www.heinemann.com

Offices and agents throughout the world

Library of Congress Cataloging-in-Publication Data
Perlmutter, Jane.
    The first weeks of school : laying a quality foundation / Jane Perlmutter, Louise Burrell.
     p.   cm.
    Includes bibliographical references.
    ISBN 0-325-00339-4 (alk. paper)
    1. Education, Elementary—Activity programs—North Carolina—Cullowhee—Case studies.
2. Project method in teaching—North Carolina—Cullowhee—Case studies.   3. Classroom environment—North Carolina—Cullowhee—Case studies.   4. Cullowhee Valley Elementary School (Cullowhee, N.C.)   I. Burrell, Louise.   II. Title.
LB1592 .P47   2001
372.1102—dc21

                                       00-050564

Editor: Danny Miller
Production: Sonja S. Chapman
Cover design: Jenny Jensen Greenleaf
Manufacturing: Louise Richardson

Printed in the United States of America on acid-free paper

04 03 02   DA   2 3 4 5

To my family—especially my parents, my husband Dan, my children Sarah, Sam, and Jason, my wonderful grandsons Dylan and Devin.

Jane

To my husband Frank and my son Marc for their unending patience, total support, and their willingness to always help me.

Louise

And to all the children and the teachers who care for them.

Contents

Acknowledgments

Special thanks go from both of us to: our parents who taught us about caring and learning; our families who have been patient, listened, encouraged, and read the story; Danny, a great editor, whose insightful comments made the book work; Frank for typing the bibliography and all those charts; Ella who helped make the classroom possible; all the Busy Bees who are the heart of the story; all the parents of the children in Louise's room who volunteered in the room and all those who supported and encouraged her; Lester who encouraged us to tell the story; Gloria who made us believe we could do it; Katie who told us to start with stories; Ruth who provided resources and encouragement; Michael who kept asking if it was done yet; Norma who has inspired us both over many years; and Shirley who kept everything going.

Louise sends special thanks to all the people who have supported her on her journey: especially A. J. Rudd, Bruce Henderson, Ada Setzer, and the people at NCCAT. Thanks to Doris, her sister, for their thirty-five years of discussions on education and to Margaret Nations who was her first wonderful teaching assistant.

Jane thanks her good friends and colleagues who have encouraged her—Terry, Lisa, and Karen. She especially thanks Shirley, Carol, and Mary Lou for being wonderful friends and great listeners. She couldn't have done any of it without their support.

Introduction

The beginning of school is both exciting and anxiety provoking for children and their teachers. The smell and feel of new notebooks, backpacks, and school clothes makes August and September a time full of promise. The first weeks of school lay the foundation for the whole school year. For beginning teachers and those teachers who want to transform their teaching approaches to create child-centered classrooms, the question of how to begin the school year is crucial.

What happens in the early days and weeks of school can create a caring, responsible community in a smoothly running classroom or can produce a jumble where the children and the teachers are at odds and may even clash with each other. Attention paid to the concepts of community, character, and quality at the beginning of the school year saves time and effort throughout the year.

This book tells the story of how one teacher, who taught her children in extraordinary ways, began her school year. Before I introduce this teacher, I need to explain who I am and how I came to know her story.

Jane's Story

I went into education backward. My undergraduate degree was in psychology but my heart was in child development. Two years teaching in the Peace Corps broadened my worldview and increased my curiosity about how children learn. Coming home, I found a job teaching kindergarten. I loved the children I taught with a passion and I wanted to facilitate their learning, not be their boss or dictator. I wanted children to learn and explore for the joy of discovery. However, keeping wiggley five-year-olds still enough for story time was a challenge for me as a new teacher.

As part of my graduate work in education I found, almost by accident, rich, exciting reports of schools that met the needs of children. Descriptions of the British Infant Schools and their American counterparts offered glimpses of the way I wanted to work with children. According to these reports, these children were free to pursue their own interests and seemed to learn almost effortlessly in authentic environments. I was hooked. The children learned because they wanted to, not because they were coerced or forced.

My vision of schools where children work for the love of learning and where children learn to coexist as a caring group was always in my mind when I taught and when I studied about teaching. Over the years the children I taught provided fascination and frustration for me, but I could never quite create the classroom I envisioned.

When I moved to the mountains of North Carolina to take a university teaching job at Western Carolina University in 1988, I began to hear about a primary classroom where young children actually *played* and *learned*.

Louise's Story

I went to visit that class and met the teacher, Louise Burrell. She is now retired but taught children in Alaska for four years and then taught for more than thirty years in the mountains of western North Carolina. Louise taught the last ten years at Cullowhee Valley Elementary School, located about two hours from the western border of the state.

The population of families at Cullowhee Valley School is a mix of "locals," people with deep roots in the Appalachian culture, and university people who work at the local regional university. The people are mainly white. A few African-American children attend the school and some children with university connections come from far-away countries. Many families in the area claim some Cherokee ancestry. Most of the children come from modest homes. No one is particularly rich.

Living in a rural area has advantages and disadvantages for children. Most of them can explore the outdoors amidst the beauty of the mountains. Despite the rural nature of the area, the larger world is available in most people's living rooms through cable or satellite dish. Rural America is no longer comfortably isolated from the outside world.

In Louise's classroom I found what I had been looking for. Children worked and played in harmony together. They had a say in their work. With Louise they formed a democratic community where each person had a voice. They learned to read and write and do math. They pursued projects based on their interests. They were excited about what they discovered and they shared their learning eagerly. They played and worked in sand, water, dramatic play, clay, and woodworking.

"How does she do that?" This question resonated with other questions I had from my first kindergarten classroom. Over the past ten years, I have been seeking the answer to the question of how she did it. Every time I went into Louise's classes, I found something new and exciting.

In Louise's class I saw a vision of what could be. Her philosophy in practice was revolutionary. It changed lives. If other teachers could embrace this way of teaching, we could create and nurture children who could save this wobbly world of ours. We need children who care and are responsible for themselves, each other, and their environment. We need children who can tackle and solve everyday problems, because then they will be prepared to solve those big world problems that will be their inheritance. We need children who get along with each other, who resolve arguments with words, not force, and who understand consensus.

Telling the Story

Several years ago, I decided to take an ethnographic look at how Louise developed her classroom. With necessary permissions in hand, I went to school. I was not able to go every day; I had to continue teaching my university classes. I went several times a week especially at the beginning of the year. I scribbled field notes furiously on legal pads. I talked to kids and participated in class activities. I helped out where I was needed but generally tried to fade into the background. At the end of the year when I discussed telling the story with the children, I asked them to each select a pseudonym. The names in the story are the names that the children chose.

Since that year of observation, Louise and I have collaborated to tell this story using my observational notes and Louise's interpretations and memories. Throughout the narrative where there are no quotation marks, I am relating my observations. Louise's direct comments and reflections are in shaded boxes throughout the story.

Teacher's Questions

Louise Burrell is unique in our area. There are teachers in nearby towns who want to come and spend a month with her. Teachers come from all over the state to spend a day or two. A day or two is all most busy teachers can realistically manage. Unfortunately teachers are rarely allowed the learning and growing time they crave. The teachers who come have the "why" in their hearts and want to know the "hows." How does this begin? How do children learn to be independent and self-directed? How are they held accountable? How are they assessed? How does this fit with the state standard course of study?

It is difficult to answer questions like these in a day's visit or an hour's presentation. This book is the story of Louise Burrell and the classroom she constructed during the first weeks of school. This is also the story of her very wise assistant, Ella Ensley, and the care and guidance she gave to the children. And most of all, this is the story of the children who struggled, learned, and grew from August to June, from shaky beginnings to confident self-reliant endings. This story of the beginning of a year in Louise's class does not lay out a recipe for what to do on Monday or Tuesday. The adaptations that can be made are up to each risk-taking teacher.

Beliefs About Children and Learning

In this book Louise and I describe how she began the school year in ways that helped children develop into independent, responsible, and caring people. We tell how Louise helped her primary children learn to produce quality work in a classroom community. We believe that classrooms should be built on principles such as freedom of expression and responsibility. Children should be encouraged to voice their opinions as long as they respect and honor the rights of others. This means that they may even disagree with their teacher. Classroom communities should be designed to allow children to make choices and decisions while accepting the responsibilities that go with them. Classrooms need to be characterized by a sense of fairness. The same expectations should apply to all children, regardless of family background, wealth, or connections. For classroom communities to function well, a sense of caring must pervade the group. Our country was founded by people who were risk takers willing to try new things. In a healthy classroom community, the children's spirit of adventure and risk taking is nurtured not crushed.

What do you want for yourself and for the children in your classroom? What do you believe about how children learn? What do you see as the role of a teacher? What are your goals as a teacher? We believe that as a teacher, you must clarify and organize your own beliefs about children and the ways they learn best before deciding how to organize your classroom and begin working with your students. If you have a deep commitment to developing the whole child in a classroom community, then we think you will find this book useful. If you want your children to work to the best of their abilities, develop habits of caring, responsibility, and acquire a love of learning, then this book is for you. If you want to truly enjoy children and teaching, then read this book. While Louise's experience was mostly in the primary grades, we believe the theory and practice in this book is applicable to all elementary grade levels.

Theory and Practice

Our beliefs and Louise's practices stem from both experience and research. Both of us love to read and we especially love to read about education and how to create good schools for children. Our underlying paradigm is constructivist and progressive. Dewey was one of the first to argue that education flows from life experiences and must be relevant to students. Both of us read about the British Infant Schools and Open Education in the seventies. A. S. Neil and *Summerhill* (1960) challenged and fascinated us. Caroline Pratt in *I Learn from Children* (1970) gave us a glimpse of child-centered education based on Dewey's teaching, which resonated with our own understanding. Glasser (1998) confirmed our beliefs that children work best when they are participants in their learning and have control over their lives. Boyer's *The Basic School* (1995) painted a picture of what education could be. Piaget helped us see that children are not miniature adults who just need knowledge poured in, but that children are active seekers of information and constructors of knowledge. Ken Goodman, Donald Graves, Frank Smith, Nancie Atwell, and Lucy Calkins are among the many who have influenced us. In *Best Practice* (1998), Zemelman et al. reaffirm the validity of all these progressive ideals. We believe that these theorists and practitioners must be considered because they provide a vision of what education can be.

The underlying construct that flows through all these theories and practices (and goes beyond academics such as reading and writing) is that children must be empowered. True education stems from children who build on their interests and experiences. A great writing or reading program is not enough. Children must be allowed to be thinkers and doers who care about other people and who feel that they can make a difference in their world. They need to be risk takers and critical, creative thinkers who can problem solve.

We believe that integrated strategies for teaching reading, mathematics, and the writing process are excellent approaches to educating children, but that they cannot stand alone. These strategies are parts of a totality that is based on the need to empower children and give them a voice in their education. Community, character, and quality are underlying structures that make learning possible and successful. Everything that happens in a classroom is integrated. It is difficult to pull out individual parts and systems and use them successfully in isolation.

This is a book for classroom teachers and for those who teach them. We want to speak to new teachers—particularly those teachers whose teacher education programs have prepared them for integrated teaching. Often our students in teacher education programs embrace the ideals we teach but find implementation difficult in traditional schools.

We want to reach experienced teachers who see other possibilities in teaching, who strive for continuous improvement, and who want guidance for making their visions reality. Over the past ten years we have made numerous presentations and talked to many teachers about Louise's classroom. We have shown slides of children at work and samples of their creations. Teachers who see the beauty and power in Louise's teaching want to know how to develop a similar style. They often start with the fundamentals: They ask how she set up the room for learning and how she organized her materials. They want to know how she began the school year. They crave information about how to monitor the children's work and their development.

There are so many conflicting messages in education that teachers often follow other people's dictates rather than trusting their own knowledge, listening to their children, and following their hearts. We want to share with teachers how Louise laid the foundations for her classroom as she charted her own course based on what she knew about children. Louise got results by following her heart. We have faith that all teachers who have the knowledge, abilities, and desires can create the classrooms that nurture the development of the whole child. We hope this book will give teachers the tools and a little nudge to help them move forward.

1

Before School Begins: Planning for the Year

The life which is not examined is not worth living.

—PLATO

When visitors walked into Louise Burrell's class at any time during the year, they noticed self-directed and self-reliant children. Children had tasks to do and they worked quietly with concentration. They worked in different areas of the room and at their own pace. Children worked together harmoniously and when problems arose, the children often solved them without adult intervention. If visitors were able to stay for a day or two, they might have seen children in a council meeting solving a range of problems as part of their class community. If visitors had looked even more closely, they would have seen children taking responsibility for the room and for each other. Each child had a voice and a part in governing the class. Each child learned to take part in controlling his or her own learning.

Behind the Scenes

What visitors did *not* see is that it took a lot of planning and effort to teach children how to work independently and how to live as part of a democratic community. Louise worked to create a community in her classroom and taught responsibility through joint decision making, choice, and accountability. In many different problem solving situations—one-on-one, group sharing, and council meetings—children learned that they had control over themselves, their environment, and their learning as well as responsibility for taking care of the room, themselves, and each other. At the same time, the development of character within each child was greatly increased as they worked toward developing integrity, honesty, caring, dependability, and persistence.

Before telling you how Louise planned for the year, I want to take you inside her room so that you can see how the community functioned to help solve problems. The physical environment was designed before the school year began and the foundation was established with the children in the first weeks of school. To illustrate how her planning produced the atmosphere she wanted for children, I will share the story of a little boy named Tim.

Tim was a second grader with dimples, brown curls, and sparkling eyes who charmed his way into and out of all kinds of things. He was identified as having a learning disability and was pulled out of the classroom daily for special education services. In his regular classroom, the children had a little notebook where they jotted down their homework and recorded their readings and work. The children had to store their book bags in a closet in the hall. The first thing each morning they were responsible for bringing in their homework bags and putting them in a large brown tub to be checked by the assistant.

At the beginning of the year, Tim took his bag home with him every day but the homework never got back to school with him. Over time, however, with his mother's help, the homework bag managed to get back to school and into the coat closet in the hall. However, once it got to the coat closet, Tim couldn't seem to remember to take his homework out of his book bag and bring it into the classroom.

Tim's classmates met as a council to help Tim with his homework problem. The children came up with a list of different suggestions from which Tim was to choose one to help him with his problem. Tim's choice was that whoever was out by the closet when he came to school in the morning would remind him to bring in his book bag. The children were pleased with themselves and considered the problem solved.

However, the next morning when Tim came into the room he didn't have his homework book. Louise called an emergency council meeting to find out what had happened. Obviously, the problem hadn't been solved. Tim stood in front of the council and explained to its members that when he came to school, he had his homework with him but since no one was in the hall to remind him, he had forgotten to bring it into the room. The children were shocked that their plan had failed. They sat in the council circle thinking about what they could do. How could they help Tim remember his homework? They needed a new plan.

After some conversation one child finally said, "Let's put up a big sign that says, 'Tim, remember to bring in your homework bag.'" And then someone else said, "No, Tim's not the only one that forgets. Why should it just be Tim?" Eventually, the students decided to put up a big sign for everybody that said, "Please remember to bring in your homework bag, the book you read at home, and anything else you need." They made the sign and taped it to the door outside on the closet. From then on, Tim and the rest of the children remembered to bring their homework bags into the room. These wise children did a beautiful job of solving a problem and helping a friend with dignity and respect.

Louise's Reflections

Working cooperatively to help solve a personal, as well as a classroom problem, was a big step toward the evolution of the working, caring community I wanted to develop. Also, this process of solving problems and making choices and decisions empowered my children. I could see their empowerment when I observed their attitudes toward the room, other children, and themselves. When my children were empowered they were able to draw on and further develop their intrinsic motivation.

What happens at the beginning of the school year lays the foundation for the rest of the year. First consider what happens before the beginning—the planning that takes place before the children ever set foot in the classroom. This reflective, careful planning takes time and energy but it pays off when the class runs smoothly throughout the year.

Things to Consider Before School Begins

- Delve into professional books to hone your thinking about curriculum and teaching strategies.
- Reflect on the systems and procedures used in the past. Scrutinize each part carefully to find ways to improve.
- Formatively evaluate record-keeping systems you plan to use.
- Begin planning before the official teacher preparation days.
- Organize the environment to allow and encourage the children to work independently. Think through the environment by listing the learning areas you plan to include and set up the physical arrangement of the room.

- Select the books that you plan to read with the children to help develop the community at the beginning of the year.
- Select and arrange materials to catch the interests of the children when they first enter the class.
- Pay attention to the aesthetics of the room.
- Collect work samples from previous years' classes to use as examples for your new class.
- Get fired up—it's going to be a great year!

Delve into professional books to hone your thinking about curriculum and teaching strategies.

Louise started early and began her planning at home. She believes in continuous improvement and continuous learning. Teachers must be lifelong learners if they are to inspire children to adopt learning as a permanent habit. Louise loves books about teaching. She found new books and new ideas each year. She reads voraciously and finds something exciting in almost everything she reads. She has always carried books in a little book bag to read as she waited for her son or her husband to complete their various activities such as ball practice or meetings. Exploring professional books was one way Louise got excited about school each year. She collected and organized her professional books so they would be available when needed. Many were chosen to help her develop specific assignments as the year progressed, while others were for self-motivation and assessment.

Each year's planning fell into patterns. Even before going to school and setting up her room, her first step was to organize her professional books for the beginning of the year. She looked for ideas that would help her children become self-directed and active. She knew that all children could learn, but that multiple strategies were necessary. She has collected a vast array of books that deal with teaching. Over the years, she has "prowled through them" enough to know which books have ideas that would work for her. She has highlighted extensively to mark ideas she wanted to go back to. Most of her favorite books are quite yellow with highlights on the inside. Each year she added new books to the collection to help her expand the scope of her teaching. She reflected on curriculum and the changes she planned to make. She kept the state's curriculum framework firmly in mind and developed a clear sense of the various ways children in the same age range would respond to the required curriculum. Her aim was for children to learn the information they were supposed to learn while developing habits of mind to make good decisions and want to continue learning. One of Louise's favorite books for help-

ing her to reflect on her teaching and for improving her strategies for thinking and assessment was *Thinking for Themselves: Developing Strategies for
Reflective Learning* by Jeni Wilson and Lesley Wing Jan (1993).

**Reflect on the systems and procedures used in the past.
Scrutinize each part carefully to find ways to improve.**

Louise used a blank book each year to record what happened day by day
throughout the year. Daily and sometimes weekly, Louise and her assistant
recorded reflections and thoughts about what she and her children were doing. Her planning books included topics from group discussions, comments
about changes in forms or systems, remarks about things that did not go well
and needed changing, and comments from university students doing
practicum experiences in her classroom. Parents' feedback was also included.
These books provided valuable data for planning for the following year.

Louise's Reflections

I like getting feedback from as many people as possible because I learn from
other people's thoughts and experiences. It makes me a stronger teacher.
But you have to be willing to listen and be open minded. Even when the
feedback is uncomfortable, you have to be willing to go beyond your current thinking and embrace new possibilities.

As she prepared at the beginning of each year, Louise picked up one resource book at a time and skimmed through it to remind herself of ideas that
she had found useful. When specific needs arose, Louise searched for ways to
help each child, and often her books were waiting with helpful information.
Books on graphing usually came first. *I See What You Mean* (Moline, 1995), a
book about graphic organizers, gave her more ideas for assignment prompts.
Graphic organizers like charts and graphs provide tools for children to show
their work in many ways. She took a section like "Simple Diagrams" and
thought about how she could adapt the author's suggestions. She never copied
anything exactly. Everything had to fit into the classroom she was developing
to meet the needs of the specific children each year. Each year and each group
of children were different.

Nothing was accepted without reflection. She knew how important
it was to develop systems or organizational structures for the children's

work. She looked for certain books on her shelf for help. The book *I See What You Mean* has good examples of diagrams, such as the parts of a body, but there are other things Louise wanted her children to include in their work. Improvement requires consideration of earlier attempts. Several years ago she taught the children to create a chart or a diagram one step at a time. She would introduce one step, have the children practice it, and then add other steps. She noticed that the step the children were taught to do at the beginning was usually what they tended to use even after receiving further instructions. They seemed to find it difficult to integrate new steps into their working plans. This year, she planned to introduce the process as a whole and then go back over the parts as necessary, gradually polishing the work to a higher standard. She wanted the children to date their work from the first assignments. She planned to begin by having the children construct an explanatory key the first time they made a diagram, rather than waiting until the children mastered simpler steps.

Louise's Reflections

Empowering children means giving them tools to express themselves. I created a variety of open-ended assignments for my children to do. When the children responded to their assignments, I was able to easily assess their needs. Students did most of their work in blank spiral-bound recording books. The beauty of the student recording books was that I had all their work in one place and I could easily track progress. When I looked through their books and examined their work, I saw what kinds of feedback I needed to provide for each child.

She planned to wait until later in the year to introduce other kinds of graphic organizers, such as line graphs and scale diagrams. While Louise believed that every child could learn, she was also tuned into children's developmental patterns. Scale diagrams were to be delayed until November. Even in November, the children would not be expected to completely understand the concept of scale but they would begin to talk about it and use it in context with vocabulary dealing with scale. After working on measurement, the concept of scale might begin to make sense to some of the children. There were books in the art area that illustrated drawing to scale. Many of her books had ideas that would help children learn the tools of mathematics, science, and social studies needed to do their projects. Having a repertoire of tools to draw from would allow the children to create their own projects later in the year.

Louise's Reflections

I want the children to embrace tools like charts, graphs, and posters to use in the development of their projects. I knew that I would need to teach them how to do these things—they wouldn't automatically know how to construct them.

Formatively evaluate record-keeping systems you plan to use.

Having the children direct much of their work and complete open-ended assignments made good record-keeping a must. Louise had to keep track of each child's work to be sure that each child was progressing well. Systems of joint record-keeping had to be developed because it would have been impossible for the teacher to do it all. As children learned how to keep their own records, they developed responsibility, had voices in what they were learning, and came to understand how they learned best.

Louise found things in many books and took from each what was needed at the time. *In the Company of Children* by Joanne Hindley (1996) focuses on the reading and writing workshop, but Louise was particularly interested in the various ways Hindley kept track of what the children were learning. This book helped Louise reflect on what she did last year and helped her update her systems for record-keeping. She considered changing her reading log. Previously, the children kept a running record of books they had read. Now she saw the need for two parts to the reading log: a list of books and a commentary on some of them. She wanted to continue having the children record books they had read, as well as keep a record of their selection patterns. She wanted to be sure they learned to select books from different genres and of varying levels. Every year, Louise modified classroom tools like the reading logs. Her most recent class used a dialogue journal and a reading log. The reading log consisted of a chart where the children had to classify the book according to genre and to rate the book according to how they felt about it. The dialogue journal provided a place to react to some books in more detail while communicating with a partner. This interaction gave the children a real audience for their work. These processes also gave the children opportunities to read, write, and record information in a variety of ways.

One of the books that influenced Louise's system for developing children's writing was *Writing: Teachers and Children at Work* by Donald Graves (1983). His later books, *Experiment with Fiction* (1989) and *Investigate Nonfiction* (1989), helped her develop the reading chart for her children.

Louise and the children developed systems to use at the beginning of the year that could be modified when they perceived a need later in the year. For example, the children and teachers developed systems for leader of the day, cleanup, projects, book sharing, woodworking, the classroom government, and cooking. As the children used the systems during the year, they offered suggestions for improvement. With well-designed systems, the room ran smoothly. Every year Louise and her assistant, Ella, reconsidered the best places to turn in work, publishing, and homework. They decided on a large, brown plastic laundry basket that would sit near the front of the room to hold the homework bags.

Begin planning before the official teacher preparation days.

Every year Louise began getting ready for school before many of her colleagues. Even after more than thirty years of teaching, she was excited and full of new plans. The allotted work days at the beginning of the school year were never enough for Louise; she needed time prior to those few official, hurried teacher work days to contemplate and consider what she was going to do. She usually tried to begin about two weeks early. The extra time allowed her to work at an unhurried pace so that she would feel fresh on the first day of school. She obtained permission to work in her classroom from the janitor and principal. This planning time helped her set the foundation for the whole year. This early planning time also paid off in time saved during the year as systems ran smoothly. Her principal let her exchange extra days spent at the beginning of the year for optional teacher work days later in the year.

Think through by listing the learning areas you plan to include and set up the physical arrangement of the room.

Louise always started the actual process of room arrangement before school started. The room environment was complex. Before putting the furniture in place she considered all the centers or learning areas she wanted to include. The placement of each area, as well as the materials in the area, would affect the operation of the systems in the room. On her first trip into the room she simply sat in a chair and "dreamed" her room. "I tried to envision how I wanted the traffic to flow. I tried to decide on an appropriate working station for my assistant for conferences," she said. The underlying consideration was how to best utilize the space. While Louise made decisions of ways to begin the year, every room arrangement was a work in progress throughout the year. As the children used materials, problems and needs for adjustment arose. Many times during the year, furniture was shifted and materials moved. Every new school year presented the opportunity to reconsider all the elements of the room. "Every year, I corrected some flaws and in the process created new ones."

Louise's Reflections

Ella and I didn't have teacher's desks. They took up too much space and usually became collection tables for materials. We had trays and mailboxes like the children did. We kept record books about children's work in plastic organizers. They sat out of the way on a cabinet or shelf, where we could get to the material easily. We had two two-drawer file cabinets—one was for us and the children used the other one for storing their portfolios. The file cabinets became part of the "walls" that defined the learning areas. The tops of the cabinets held terrariums and aquariums that would have been in the way on tables. We did our work with children all over the room.

Packing up at the end of each school year and starting fresh at the beginning of the next was important to Louise. Years ago she decided that every year at the end of school she would pack every bit of teaching material and begin the next year afresh. Every year for more than thirty years she had done just that. At the end of each school year, she and the children boxed and labeled and sorted all the paraphernalia that made up their room. The room for the following year was created anew from bits and pieces of all kinds of things. This kept her fresh and kept her room from becoming stagnant.

Louise built her room bit by bit for over thirty years. She did not have and did not want a collection of desks for her children. She did have a collection of assorted tables of various sizes and chairs enough to seat all the children if necessary. The primary sand table, the woodworking bench, the mailboxes, the large shelving unit (which holds the old bread trays that serve as cubbies for the children's possessions) were all precious and part of the structure of her room.

Louise's Reflections

I always need at least a day to rearrange furniture. If you are smart you go around and measure the spots and check before you move it. I wish I could have the children help each year. This is a great math workout. After I go away and come back, I see other things that may need changing. I walk around and check to see if there is room for the children to walk. If the chairs are pulled out back to back, is there still room to get between them?

Organize the environment to allow and encourage the children to work independently.

The learning areas or centers were central to the development of the curriculum. Before moving the furniture, Louise listed the areas she planned to include and looked at her state curriculum guide to be sure that all areas of the curriculum were covered. Materials available help determine the learning areas that a teacher will use for any one year. Teachers just beginning to use learning areas need to include at least some basic centers to provide choice and variety and meet children's developmental needs. Basic centers for primary classrooms include reading, writing, listening, art, math, science, social studies, games, building, and dramatics. Too few centers can create problems; teachers need at least enough to take care of twenty-five to twenty-eight children in a class. Each year more centers can be added. Louise advises beginning with however many you feel comfortable with. When she first organized her room into learning areas, she did not have sand, water, cooking, sewing, or carpentry. She added one of these new learning areas each year.

Learning areas need to be defined so that children know where to work and how to find needed materials. Having a clear purpose and structure in the environment can create an underlying sense of order. Children need to live in a predictable, organized environment where everything has a place. Knowing where to locate necessary materials gives children the sense that they belong in the room and gives them a feeling of control and ownership. See Figure 1–1 for an example of Louise's classroom floor plan.

Many things can help divide the room into areas. Bookshelves, portable blackboards, pegboards, chart racks, and other screens can all serve as dividers. Rectangular tables can also divide areas. Thick corrugated cardboard can be put between two tables to separate areas.

Teachers are often advised to group noisy areas together. However, Louise has found that strategies such as putting carpet under blocks on the shelves and on the floor in the building area can reduce noise levels. Teaching children to be aware of the noise they make and to care about disturbing others also makes the conventional wisdom of separating quiet and noisy centers less crucial.

Louise's Reflections

I worry when I go into a quiet classroom. I'm afraid that learning isn't taking place when children are always expected to be quiet. When children work in learning areas, I know there will be working noise. Children develop communication skills, both written and oral, only when they have

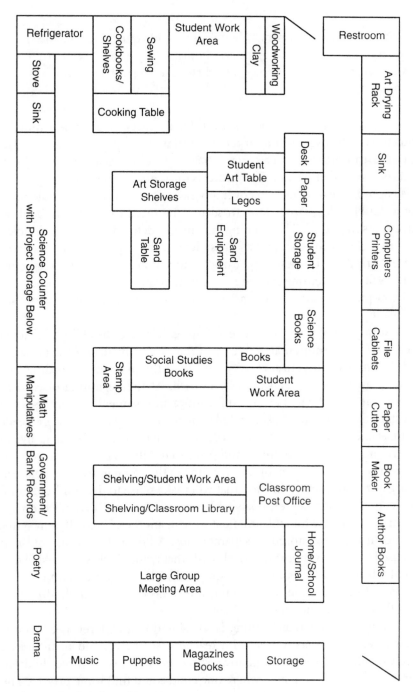

Figure 1–1. *Louise's floor plan.*

a chance to talk and interact. In this process of communicating they learn to respect the rights and opinions of others. As they talk they learn to use self-control, to care, and to express themselves in positive ways.

Messy areas need to be on uncarpeted spaces, if possible. Sometimes linoleum can be used over a carpeted area if no uncarpeted space is available. The art area works best on a surface that can be easily cleaned. Carpet on top of carpet is another option. This protects the school carpet (and keeps principals happy). Use duct tape to cover any raw edges on carpet or linoleum and use a double stick carpet tape to secure the piece to the floor. Bookcases can cover some edges. The opening into an area defined by a piece of linoleum or carpet should be as small as possible and the edges must be secured to prevent tripping. Interestingly, carpet under water and sand areas actually works well by preventing tracking of sand and water all over the room. Putting an extra piece of carpet over the bare floor or over the school carpet saves on cleanup.

At the end of every school year, Louise, Ella, and the children clean and pack up the classroom materials so that they are ready for the next class. She had the children organize, classify, and label the materials according to the learning area where they would be housed. At the beginning of each new school year after she had arranged furniture and planned the centers, Louise just started opening the boxes and placing materials where they were needed. Many elements had to be considered: "Can the children reach it easily? Can they return it easily? Is there a good place to use it?" A lid keeps the dust out but also keeps the children out. Everything in the room must have a place and be organized and sorted in ways that will make sense to the children. For example, in the water center, boats and ships for dramatic play filled one tub, and materials to use for sink and float were in another. Two different systems for measuring were stored in separate tubs. All over the room, Louise and Ella used bricks to support narrow boards that made single storage shelves on top of tables. Each work area was equipped with tools for children to use as needed. The aim for the room arrangement was to empower children to use what they needed when they needed it.

Louise believes that learning is social and that children need to interact with each other as well as with teachers, so shelves and furniture purposely divided the room into many cozy corners for two or three children to work. There were also places where one child could find some privacy. There was a large space for the whole group to gather for instruction or council meetings.

Louise's Reflections

I've found that if children feel a part of and value their working areas, they will work hard to develop the self-control they need to use them. They become very protective of the classroom as a whole. Children will watch to be sure that their friends are taking care of the materials in the class. They expect to see quality in the efforts of everyone. Peer pressure plays an important part in helping children develop self-control. Some children who tune out adult voices will listen to their peers.

Description of Learning Areas

Group Meeting Area, Books, and Games

The classroom had a large group meeting area where the children and their teachers could gather for instruction, whole group discussions, either teacher or student led, and council meetings. A chalkboard or white board needed to be accessible to the teacher and the group for recording results of meetings, outlining tasks to be done, and giving examples of work. The meeting area also served as the main part of the classroom library and was filled with books of all kinds. Louise's books, collected over many years, included series of children's favorites like *Box Car* and *American Girls,* science books organized by topic, easy readers, and chapter books. Her large collection was lovely but is not essential. Teachers' personal collections can grow and be supplemented. Libraries have books to be borrowed. Parents will donate materials and yard sales are good sources for school materials. The listening center was at a table near the far wall. Books and tapes were available for children to listen to undisturbed.

The bookshelves that formed the main part of the classroom library and the puppet stage defined the group area. The feeling was of a room within a room. After the morning group activities were completed, this area was used for many purposes. Louise stored games and puzzles on shelves near the group area so children could use the space to work and play games with friends. This space was large enough for the teachers to meet with individuals or small groups while other children were working. The puppet stage and dramatic play materials (including musical instruments) needed to be nearby so that actors and puppeteers had a place for their audiences to sit. Later in the year this space could accommodate project presentations and large group sharing. During the "Drop Everything and Read" (DEAR) time all other areas in the room were closed and many children liked to get comfortable on the carpet and read. Some of the reading groups also would find a spot in the meeting area during small group reading time.

Publishing Area

While the children wrote in all areas of the room, the writing/publishing area housed the special materials needed for the final step of the writing process—publishing. This area had two computers, a printer, paper, and supplies. Within the area various "pictionaries," dictionaries, thesauruses, and books related to writing and publishing were available for reference. Staplers, colored pencils, magic markers of varying colors and sizes, scissors, a big box of crayons, writing pens, and sticky pads all encouraged children to write and illustrate their work. An organizer with drawers held erasers, white-out, hole reinforcers, and paper clips. A child-safe paper cutter and book-binding machine were accessible to the children. Some paper was special and could only be used for publishing. Children should be able to find and use whatever they need to produce their final products. Having special supplies like new crayons and markers often enticed the children to produce their best work.

Math and Science Area

Children worked on math and science all over the room in all the learning areas. They sorted and classified with plastic vehicles and animals. They estimated length, width, and distance as they did art projects, built with blocks, or worked in carpentry. Cooking and selling the food provided much practice in math and science. In addition, specific materials for math and science were housed in tubs on shelves in the math and the science areas. Some things like a timer and rulers were used for both. They were sorted and labeled. These materials were tools that the children could take anywhere in the room to use. Shelves in the math area held color cubes, unifix cubes, cuisenaire rods, geometric shapes, pattern blocks, pattern cards, rubber bands, geoboards, money stamps, and assorted geometric shapes. Most of the science materials such as batteries, wires, tuning forks, color paddles, magnets, clocks, thermometers, and magnifying equipment were used later in the year for specific projects. Children were expected to make plans for their use. The math materials were used daily, often with investigation work in groups or independently.

Rubber Stamps

On another shelf, which also housed reference books, Louise arranged a station for using stamps. Some stamps were specifically for math, like money stamps, unifix stamps, clocks, thermometer stamps, and shapes. There were also stamps of animals, people, flowers, and dinosaurs. Stamps and stamp pads could be used for decoration and discovery. Templates for producing fancy lettering or various shapes were also available. Children used these stamps for all kinds of projects. Children created borders around their work and decorated their products for presentation.

Social Studies Area

A globe, compasses, maps, and many books provided tools for some of the work in social studies. This area was used to display artifacts from other countries at various times during the year. At the same time, the whole classroom served as a laboratory for the development of values, problem solving strategies, and social skills.

Each of these learning areas had appropriate books on display and for reference. The books were changed throughout the year to stimulate new interests. Displays of sample work also motivated and informed the children to countless possibilities.

Art Area

The art area required a good table for construction work, bookcases to house materials for construction, containers for supplies like paste, markers, rulers, and scissors. Various sizes, colors, and types of paper needed to be readily available. Tubs or dish pans held recycled materials such as paper towel tubes, styrofoam packing materials, yarn, popsicle sticks, rocks, seeds, small pieces of cloth, colored tissue paper, empty containers of all sorts, boxes, and box lids. All these materials stimulated creativity and problem solving and allowed children to make anything they needed in their work. The art area included easel painting, clay, Creation Station, and "beautiful junk." The clay table with its clay board, closed bucket for clay storage, and materials for working the clay was an important part of the art center. The easel needed to have various sizes of paper, smocks for cover-up, and specially labeled cleaning cloths.

Blocks and Construction Materials Area

The block area had blocks, Legos, plastic/rubber models of farm and wild animals, and cars and trucks for dramatic play. The center was enclosed on three sides by bookcases and provided a private place for constructive and dramatic play with the various building materials. The block area needed to be protected and out of the main traffic flow. Children did not like their constructions bumped and disturbed. Enclosure and protection honored the children and respected the work they did. Other construction materials like Legos were good to build with and some constructions could be motorized. Large boards could be used to make inclined planes for experimenting. Blocks needed to be classified and labeled according to shapes and sizes. Two tubs of Tinker Toys and small pieces of paper for making signs were stored—one in the blocks and the other in sand.

Sewing Area

The sewing center also needed to be housed off the carpet because of the risk of needles or pins becoming embedded in carpet. The sewing center was both an extension of the art area and a place for children to practice patterning, geometry, measurement, and to learn new vocabulary. Parents and grand-parents were often recruited to help in this area as well as in woodworking and cooking. Each child would have a personal, labeled small plastic bag contain-ing a needle and special material such as plastic sewing frames and pieces of fabric. Each needle was stored in an empty plastic cassette holder. Other con-tainers could be used but the container should be see-through. Louise usually checked these visually later in the year to be sure the needles were stored safely. These plastic bags with their carefully stored needles were kept in a tub in the sewing center. For safety reasons, the children would not be allowed to carry needles to other parts of the room. Yarn and thread were stored in another tub along with buttons, thimbles, needle threaders, scissors, and pinking shears (to make edges that will not fray). Another tub held pieces of lace and other trim for decorating projects. In order to be sure the scissors and shears re-mained sharp, they were reserved for use in the sewing centers and children were not allowed to take them to cut paper.

Woodworking Area

While many classrooms don't have woodworking areas, Louise found a wood-working center to be well worth the time and investment. If possible, the woodworking area should be near an outside door, so that loud hammering can move outside. Lining the woodworking bench with more carpet muffled the sound of hammering. A pegboard was an excellent place to organize tools. The outline of each tool and its label organized and instructed children. Safety goggles and work gloves were a must. Woodworking was one of the last areas in the room to open, only after the children had learned about caring for the other materials in the room and each other. Woodworking with real tools to make real products required responsible children.

When children wanted to do woodworking, sewing, or cooking they were required to write plans. These areas thus provided opportunities for ap-plying reading, writing, science, math skills, as well as social studies.

Water Area

Creating a water area does not necessarily require an expensive commercial water tub. Any large plastic container, preferably one that is transparent, can enable children to engage in science experiences involving measuring, pouring, sinking, and floating as well opportunities for dramatic play and pretend. Materials need to be housed in tubs, classified, and labeled. Measuring containers, water wheels, sieves, plastic boats, tubes, a siphon, and containers of varying shapes and sizes need to be available. Materials like glass, wood, ping pong balls, lids, and metal all encourage children to find out what sinks and floats and to consider why. A clean-up tub housing sponges also needs to be readily available.

Sand Area

A sand table, like a water area, provides opportunities for math, science, language, and dramatic play. Sand allows for building and creating models for social studies. Sanitized play sand is safe and the best choice for school use. A wide flat board that fits across the sand box can make a platform for holding measuring devices or tubs of materials while the children are working. Louise did not allow tubs of materials on the bottom in the sand table because they would inevitably transfer extra sand to the shelves and onto the floor. A dustpan and small brush are also necessary tools for this center.

While older children use sand and water in more sophisticated ways than younger children do, all children delight in as well as learn from their explorations of these raw materials. Sometimes the sand and water areas can help cure the negative attitudes toward academics that plague some children. A child who has experienced failure in school may go to those areas first and find success.

Cooking Area

The cooking area needs to be close to water. If a sink is not available nearby, the children can carry buckets of water into the room. In Louise's class there was a microwave, a refrigerator, a toaster oven, and cooking equipment plus plenty of cookbooks. In her class, cooking helped the children learn to read and write and do mathematics. Teachers always kept an eye on the cooking area. Children generally were fairly independent as they worked in cooking. They knew that when they encountered certain things they needed to go get a teacher. When something sharp was used or the children used heat, the teacher or assistant would supervise more closely. A table was used for preparing and selling the food.

To create a cooking area, a space needs to be found in the class where electrical outlets are nearby. If outlets are not close, it is possible to use heavy-duty extension cords and special materials to keep small hands off the cords and water from touching them. Bookshelves and cabinets for housing supplies are necessary. A pegboard is nice but not essential for holding utensils. On a pegboard, the utensils can be labeled and arranged to show size gradations. Children can learn science, math, and cooking vocabulary in a real context.

In Louise's room, a place for advertisements, a calendar for sign-up, and a flowchart explaining the process for using the area were posted in the center. Many interested parents and people in the community donated much of the equipment for the cooking area.

Children's Storage Areas

Since the children had no assigned seats in the class and work was done at tables in the various areas, children needed several places to store their books and materials. Just beyond the art center a large bookcase stood holding old metal trays where children would put their workbooks. These were blank books where the children recorded their work. Students' storage trays (see Figure 1–2) were numbered. The teachers made sure that their names, first and last, were on the storage trays. Systems for numbering allowed children to be independent and in charge. Under the built-in cupboards were project trays, one for each pair of children. Projects were often large and cumbersome and needed safe places to be kept.

Cleaning Materials   Every year Louise bought one plain wash cloth for each student to use as a cleaning cloth. Cleaning cloths were stored in the bathroom. They were numbered and clipped to a matching numbered clothespin on a strip of wood that a parent hot glued into place on the wall in the bathroom. Clothespins numbered from one through twenty-six were attached to the strip of wood. Each child had a cleaning cloth to use at clean-up time. After they finished cleaning each day, they rinsed and wrung out their cloths. On Friday, Louise took them home to wash and bleach.

Other Storage: Post Office and Working Tools   Near the front of the classroom across from a paper center were the post office boxes where the children would send and receive mail. The working tools cabinet created one of the walls for the block center. Each child would be assigned a number and a smaller tray to hold the child's numbered pencil gripper, calculator, ruler, and a pair of number generators (dice) in a black plastic film container. These working tools were checked out to children according to the numbers and the children were responsible for keeping track of them. Numbered stray materials found around the room were *easy* to match with their owners.

Figure 1–2. *Working tool trays.*

Louise's Reflections

I worked to construct the room so that it could be used independently by the children. This saved me valuable time as I didn't have to constantly give permission, reminders, and directions. The systems that were developed with the children enabled them to work freely within the room.

Using Learning Areas or Centers

Being comfortable with learning areas depends on a teacher's beliefs about children and how children learn. Trusting children is essential to using centers. Ask yourself these questions: Do you believe that children can learn from their own efforts and from interaction with each other? Do you believe that children will be able to help manage their own learning? Do you believe that children can be motivated from within? Do you believe that children learn by doing and searching for answers? Do you believe that children can learn to problem solve? Do you believe that children can develop self-control?

Learning areas or centers create a planned environment for learning. They are much less effective if they are only used for enrichment, when there is extra time, or as a reward. They are not useful unless they are used by children. Many classrooms have wonderful areas and equipment but their use is primarily teacher directed and children rarely use the materials.

Having learning areas is not a license for permissiveness. Louise had structured and unstructured learning. The materials within each learning area, as well as the assignments that will be described later, focused the children on the curriculum. If a teacher wants to use learning areas he or she needs to consider a number of factors.

Display and Maintenance of Materials

Throughout the year, teachers need to make sure that materials are labeled, displayed neatly, and replaced when necessary. Old, broken, or unused materials left to clutter the room lead to uncaring attitudes toward the areas. Where children's work and exhibits are part of particular areas, the children and the teachers need to be sure that the displays are kept up to date.

In all learning centers or areas, materials should be labeled neatly so that students will know where to get and return the things they need. For instance, the staplers should be placed on a labeled tray or sheet of construction paper. When a stapler is needed, everyone knows where it is. Trays, mats, and containers define the proper locations for tools all over the room.

Each area should be easily accessible to children at their level. The neatness and orderliness of each area sends messages to the children that working materials are valued and respected. They are expected to keep their personal trays orderly as well.

Louise's Reflections

I wanted to help lay the foundation for their participation in the adult communities they would be part of some day. So I talked with the children about how as adults they would have to care for and respect their communities. Then I had them brainstorm ways that they could show respect, care for each other, their communities, and for the earth. They decided to try to avoid things like throwing litter out of car windows or writing on walls.

Evaluating the Use of the Areas

Children should know how to use each area, what is expected, and why. At the end of each day during the first week or so, the class needs to meet together and evaluate how they are using the areas. They should consider how they feel about using the centers, what problems are being encountered, and how improvements can be made. This is a good way to begin the process of self-evaluation. When the centers are being used smoothly, other concerns are raised in more academic areas like the writing process or reading.

Use of Space   Use of space is as important as the placement of materials. Paths around and through learning areas do not need to be wide. One person needs to be able to move through comfortably. The teacher, as well as the children, should be able to access all areas of the room. While seats are not assigned, there needs to be one chair for each person in the room.

Developing Responsibility   As children move from one area to another, they should be responsible for leaving the areas where they have been working in good order before moving to another area. At first the children may feel uncomfortable not having desks, but with personal places to keep personal materials and work, they will soon think of the entire classroom as belonging to them.

> **Select the books that you plan to read with the children to help develop the community at the beginning of the year.**

Community as Part of the Curriculum

The curriculum was built in many ways, it didn't just happen through written assignments. The community that the children and their teachers created was a major part of the curriculum. A community is created and grows when people share many things. The stories and experiences that the children and teachers shared built joint understanding. Children need opportunities to interact orally with each other and their teachers. They need to learn to listen, to disagree, and to express their opinions. A caring community provides a safe context for communication. Building community through sharing stories is one of the major building blocks in helping children grow into citizens in a democracy.

The Value of Story

Louise wanted to begin helping the children to understand democratic values, and there was no better way to do so than through a good story. Stories have power for children and leave lasting impressions in their minds. Stories stimulate thought, ignite children's imaginations, and foster their intrinsic motivation. Over the years, Louise has collected many children's books and stories that stimulated children to think and make connections between concepts. Several weeks before school began, Louise gathered and assessed her children's books to find read alouds that would establish the tone and introduce major themes for the year. She also thought about the stories she had shared with children in the past. At the beginning of school, she would read these books and tell these stories to the large group and they would discuss the books and stories together. These books led into the character curriculum for the year. Together the teacher and children would use the books to establish major themes of caring and responsibility.

When I Was Young in the Mountains (Rylant, 1982) connected to the children's Appalachian mountain environment. Louise wanted them to feel connected to their own geography as well as to the whole world. She wanted them to feel pride in their uniqueness and comfort in their common ties with the wider world. She explained, "We live in the mountains and we speak differently from people in other places." She wanted her children to realize that differences were okay. They needed to feel good about where they lived and how they talked and dressed. Shel Silverstein's *The Missing Piece* (1976) continues the lesson by telling children that it is okay to be different and to each grow in their own ways.

At some point the children needed to shift their attention from themselves to the larger world and their responsibilities for it. Bill Peat's *The Wump World* (1974) focused the children on issues like the needs of animals, plants, pollution and caring for the earth. *Dear Children of the Earth: A Letter from Home* (1994) by Schim Schimmel reinforced the necessity for taking care of our world. The children in Louise's class would gradually come to see the classroom as a small world within the larger world. They would learn to care for the larger world by working to improve the smaller world that was their class. They needed to be taught and they needed a chance to practice what they had learned. The small world of the classroom provided a place to practice for living in the larger world. These concepts were at the heart of the social studies curriculum.

In *The Missing Piece Meets the Big O* (1981), also by Shel Silverstein, the missing piece has a vision of what he wants to do. He wants to roll like the big O, but can't because of his shape. The big O assures him that trying can make a difference. The Missing Piece flops over and over and slowly turns himself into a shape that can roll. This book encourages children to make efforts and keep trying. Persistence is an old-fashioned virtue that is crucial to quality work.

Oh, the Places You'll Go! (1990) by Dr. Seuss would lead the children into discussions of what they wanted to learn about this year. Considering topics of interest would introduce the notion of finding out about things by doing projects. Reading *Peace Begins with You* (Scholes, 1989) would help the children visualize the value of community and foster their understanding of the importance of government.

Many books have messages to bring to children. While Louise planned on four or five books for the first week or so of school, her planning was flexible. When she met the children and assessed their unique needs, she might drop a book and pick up another one. The children's reactions and levels of appreciation would help her decide. Louise was always on the lookout for new children's books that illustrated lessons she wanted her children to learn.

Select and arrange materials to catch the interests of the children when they first enter the class.

When the room arrangement was in place and the materials were arranged, the next question was what to put out in the room to greet the children. Materials available in the classroom were there to stimulate oral interactions. Louise wanted children to wonder, question, and talk to each other. She wanted them to be curious and to always search for answers to the questions they generated.

Louise's Reflections

Since I knew most children like animals, I displayed a collection of books and artifacts to catch their interest. I had books about animals, bones, fossils, seashells, a bird's nest, rocks, things about the earth, and things kids like. I displayed five big carpenter bees, which had just died. I put them by the magnifying glasses. Hairy, the tarantula, had spent the summer at our house and was back in the class in a large terrarium.

The tarantula was an easy animal to care for. She required a cricket or two each week and enjoyed other creepy, crawly things the children found for her. Near Hairy's cage, Louise had some model dinosaurs and books about dinosaurs. She put out a model airplane and other transportation vehicles. Even things constructed by children from previous classes would be placed on display. An aquarium sat empty, waiting for what the children might bring to school.

Real Object Collections

Louise has been a collector for years. She kept big labeled and numbered boxes on high shelves at home or in closets at school. Sometimes kind custodians allowed her to store her boxes in their storage areas. She collected things like bones, rocks, turtle shells, dried seed pods, sea shells, models of airplanes, fossils, and arrowheads for display. Fishnets, a special doll, dried insects and butterflies—anything could become part of an interest-catching display. When children showed a particular interest, then the materials to extend their study were at hand.

Louise's Reflections

I think that part of the fun of teaching is continually searching for things that will interest children. Every time my husband Frank and I took a trip we looked for neat things to take back to the classroom. We once carried a live chipmunk all the way to Alaska because the children we were teaching had never seen chipmunks. Bones, strange seed pods, interesting rocks, a piece of wood that a beaver had gnawed, or big pieces of fungi caught my children's attention and got them excited. These items became the springboards for motivating children to want to learn about the world. When my children's parents saw these things on display, they brought in more interesting stuff. I always tried to match displays with corresponding books at different reading levels.

Pay attention to the aesthetics of the room.

Aesthetics were important. Louise believes in the importance of a pleasing, comfortable room. Beauty and order should surround children. She did not fill the walls with commercial decorations before school began. She might put up a few posters but generally she waited to put up children's work from the first day of school. She said that if she filled the walls with things adults made, the children would not feel ownership. Throughout the year, their work was carefully displayed so that it was pleasing to the eye. Displays were changed frequently and placed at children's eye level as much as possible. Displaying children's work carefully told children that their work was valuable and that they came first in this environment.

While organizing the learning areas, Louise kept the importance of beauty in mind. She did not want an environment that was so busy that it distracted children from their learning. For instance she chose blue as a unifying color. She had blue trays for children's work, predominately blue curtains, and blue mats for display. She planned neutral backgrounds for displaying children's work. Black or brown mats made their work stand out. Earth tones and soft blues seemed to have a calming effect on the children and their teachers. Every learning area and display area was planned for their appearance as well as their practical value (see Figure 1–3).

Figure 1–3. *Display area.*

Louise's Reflections

I believe that the physical environment in which we spend our days has an important effect on our mood and attitudes. I always tried very hard to make our working environment inviting, organized, and usable. I wanted to be sure that the whole room, as well as individual and group displays and exhibits, reflected care and quality. I often shopped for fabric to use in displays and I had a collection of material with different textures and patterns. I knew that I wanted to model quality and caring by taking into account consideration of color, design, arrangement of materials, and equipment. We needed our classroom to be as inviting, comfortable, and usable as a home. We spent so many of our days in the classroom that I worked to create a wonderful, desirable place for children to be.

Collect work samples from previous years' classes to use as examples for your new class.

Fostering Effort

Louise wanted each child to work to the best of his or her ability. Effort was key. Every year before school started she went back to her children's work from previous years and pulled out good quality samples and samples that did not show a lot of effort. She planned to use these several weeks into the new school year. Talking about work from previous years avoided the problems of discussing and comparing work of the children in the classroom. Louise made sure that all names on work samples were hidden so no one knew whose projects were being discussed. This way they could talk about work without hurting anyone's feelings or making anyone feel superior. Louise believes that fear impedes learning, so that the discussion of less-than-quality work must not discourage children. These samples would be the basis for developing quality indicators with the children at the beginning of the year. They discussed the quality of the work they were examining. They learned to identify the things that made work "quality" or "not quality."

Through these work samples, the children began to look at ways that work could be improved and to understand that it was okay to work at different levels. Community and respect for each other were developed as the class examined work samples. The children had to feel safe and comfortable before they could establish indicators of quality. True quality only came when there was no fear and children felt they could take risks. The children had to learn to talk, to listen, and to honor different opinions. They would also learn that "mistakes are stepping stones to learning." This helped take the fear and anxiety out of learning.

Meeting Individual Needs

Louise operated her class so that she could meet the individual needs of each child. She believed that each child should be evaluated in terms of his or her own competencies. Children came into school each year operating at diverse levels. At any grade level, some come to school reading chapter books, while others still struggle with the connections between letters and sounds. Louise wanted to leave no child behind. She knew that each child could learn if the opportunities were presented carefully. Eliminating fear and encouraging risk taking were top priorities.

Get fired up—it's going to be a great year!

After several weeks of preparation, Louise was full of energy and excitement at the prospects of a new year. The general framework of the learning environment was in place but there were still bits and pieces lying around for the children to organize.

Planning begins with a deep faith in children and a commitment to meeting their needs. Louise's philosophy has been built over the years through a combination of experience, study, and reflection. Louise planned the room and environment the way she did so that she could put her beliefs into action. The beliefs that guided her planning and practice were:

- Every child can learn and deserves the same quality instruction.
- Learning requires a child to be active, not passive.
- Learning is social and requires interaction.
- An aesthetically pleasing room sends the powerful message to children that they are important and valued.
- Empowerment creates intrinsic motivation and is created by choices, decision making possibilities, and responsibility.
- Each child is evaluated in terms of his or her own goals.
- When a child is having a problem in the classroom, the people with the best solutions are often their classmates.
- Mistakes are stepping stones to learning.
- Fear stops and impedes learning.
- Children learn what they see adults doing.

- Success breeds success.
- Character development should be integrated throughout the curriculum.
- Learning is continuous and integrated.

These beliefs were the foundation of Louise's plans for each new school year. Honoring these beliefs required a commitment to creating an environment where children had both freedom and responsibility. Turning these beliefs into reality took thought, planning, and constant reflection.

2

The First Day:
Creating Community

Knowing is not enough, we must apply. Willing is not enough, we must do.

—GOETHE

The start of school puts butterflies in stomachs. Even after weeks of getting ready, teachers wonder about what the new group of children will be like. Some veteran teachers may still have nightmares about finding themselves in strange classrooms without preparation or a clue about what to do. At the beginning of each new school year, children worry about their teachers, how they will be treated, and whether they will have friends. These anxieties mean that, for most people, the beginning of school is both exhilarating and frightening. If a teacher plans to try unfamiliar strategies and transform his or her teaching, the questions of what to do or say can be intimidating. The first day sets the tone for a year's worth of caring and work. The major work of the first days of school should be building community and letting butterflies go.

The First Day of School

Cars and children were everywhere in front of the school. The parking lots were full and cars were parked on grass and dirt almost out to the highway. The bell rang and the corridors were full of excited children. Faces were flushed with anticipation and excitement. New book bags and lunch boxes with no dirt or scratches were proudly borne down the halls.

35

Warm Welcomes

At the classroom door, Ella, the assistant teacher, stood greeting and welcoming the second-grade children as they entered. Three children stood with her, waiting for friends to arrive. Their excitement was palpable. I came in to see how the first day of school got started.

No wonder the children were excited—as soon as they approached the door they could see that the classroom was a rich environment full of promise. It was divided into learning areas or centers, each full of possibilities for exploration.

Three friends welcomed a new arrival. All over the room kids were exploring. They were careful, hands-off—not sure what would be allowed. They looked and talked with quiet excitement. It helps to know someone in this new situation. Pairs and groups of threes seemed more comfortable than individual children.

A child walked by and looked at shells and a snakeskin on display. Then he moved on to look at the live tarantula. His parents told him good-bye from the door.

Louise's Reflections

The unusual materials that I put around the room are there to capture the children's attention from the very beginning. Children are born curious. I believe that schools need to foster children's excitement and innate curiosity. Teachers need to listen to the questions their children ask and encourage them to answer their own questions. The sparkle in the eye and the desire to know—this is the magic of learning. Good teaching should begin with the children's interests. As children explore, question, and answer their own questions, their academic skills will develop more quickly and smoothly as they are interwoven in their work than with a teacher-directed paper-and-pencil approach.

Setting Limits

Two or three children began a fast walk—almost a run. Louise observed, "Oh, they are so ready to go." She moved to the fast walkers and told them gently, quietly, but firmly that they needed to slow down in the room. The children had checked out the speed limit. Louise knew the need for limits, which the children would soon set for themselves. She also understood the needs and tendencies of young children to explore. She commented to me that they were exploring trails around the room.

Two boys looked over the woodworking area, talking about and pointing out the tools. One child pulled another by the arm, "Don't make me fall," he replied. The children were cautious in their explorations. I heard one child tell another, "Be careful."

Louise told several children, "All centers are closed until we do some talking."

"Listen!" She used the word that was the signal that would be used throughout the year to get the attention of the class. She called them to the carpet to do some talking. The groups of children drifted over to the meeting area on a gentle wave of excitement.

Ella explained to the assembled children, "This is our meeting area." As the children began to sit down, Louise noticed that there was not enough space for comfortable sitting. Ella, Louise, and four children efficiently moved the five pieces of furniture a few feet back that created the divider between the large group area and the worktables. Now the group area was large enough to accommodate everyone.

On the open, carpeted space that was the meeting area, the children chatted and giggled. Louise had the children count off to see how many were there. Twenty-three children were at school this first day. She knew that two children were still on vacation.

"Did you have a good summer?"

"Yeah!" was the enthusiastic reply.

"Boy, I had a good summer. I did a lot of learning. I got to do lots of reading for fun."

The children shared some of the things they had read.

"Did you go on a trip?"

Many kids wanted to share stories of summer fun.

A Difficult Entrance

Not all children came into the room easily and comfortably. Near the door a little girl stood anxiously with her mom and a very new baby. Louise went over to talk with them. The mom needed to know about pickup in the afternoon. Then giving Kayla a kiss, she started to leave. The child asked tremulously, "Do I have to stay all day?"

Louise gave the little girl a large seashell and asked her to take it and put it next to an empty aquarium in the corner. As the child left, Louise quietly suggested that the mom could now go. The mother did not leave and before sitting down, the little girl came back and asked to give her mom a hug.

Kayla's mom had unknowingly circumvented Louise's distraction strategy for helping a reluctant child join the class. If mom had left while Kayla was putting the shell in place, tears might have been avoided.

Louise told Kayla to hug her mom and then come right back and join the circle. "We'll wait for you," she remarked encouragingly. Louise was trying to provide another chance for Kayla to slip into the class meeting.

Kayla still clung to her mother. She was new to the school, had a new stepfather, a new house, and a new baby brother. She was not ready to face a new school, new children, and new teachers.

Getting Acquainted

In the group area Louise continued, "I'm going to start with me and then Mrs. Ensley and we'll take turns telling about ourselves. My name is Mrs. Burrell. I have a husband who's a little messy but a good husband and a son who is starting his first day of high school. He had butterflies in his stomach this morning. Did any of you feel that way?"

Many of the children agreed that they, too, had butterflies.

Louise continued telling about the animals she had and then she told the children, "My favorite thing is reading and my other favorite thing is to teach. My favorite food is apples and my second favorite I'm working on changing. It's chocolate ice cream. Is there anything else you would like to know about me?"

"How old are you?" one child asked.

"Very old!" was the answer.

Just then the principal came on over the intercom. He encouraged the children to take care of the new building. "It's our responsibility. A walk through the cafeteria will begin at 9:30 with first-grade teachers who will start the process."

As he talked, one child "shushed" another. These children were aware of many school rules already.

Meanwhile, Ella talked gently to the reluctant Kayla. By now Kayla was crying and Ella suggested that she wash her face. Her mom and baby brother were still in the room. Her mom talked to her while she sobbed. The more Kayla cried, the more upset Kayla became.

Louise's Reflections

My assistant, Ella, worked with me for more than ten years. She had a great intuitive grasp of children and how to work with them. She helped organize and maintain the various systems in the room. She was an avid learner. We read books, shared tapes, and took courses together. I always had a hard time stopping children when they were really involved in their work, but she kept me on track with time. Without her, we would never have been anywhere when we were supposed to be. Perhaps most important of all, she really cared for and loved all the children.

Ella and Louise changed places. They had worked together for so long that they easily changed roles when the need arose. Ella quietly told children who were growing anxious about Kayla's crying, "Her name's Kayla. She used to go to another school. She doesn't know anyone here. Let's all be her special friend. She doesn't know anybody." Caring was the answer to many problems in this class.

Then Ella introduced herself by telling about her daughter and her six cats and two dogs.

Sharing Time

"Listen, it will be your turn to share in a minute. The magic word is 'Listen.' That means when you hear it, you stop whatever you are doing and start to listen. Now you know the magic word."

Someone wanted to know how old she was.

She laughed, "As old as dirt!"

Ella continued, "We are teachers but we have twenty-seven teachers in this room all the time. Think of yourself as a teacher. Children are so special because we learn so much from them every day."

Chris asked if you could tell something you did. "Can you tell about your relative?"

"You can tell what you want in the time you have." They decided to allot two minutes each because they did not want to sit too long. Decisions began right away on the first day.

Jax began. "I've been working on books and more books. I have a new book called *Black and White War.*" He told of his love of dinosaurs and the movie, *Jurassic Park.*

Ella told him that there would be sharing time every day and if someone brought in something special, that person could put it in the closet so it wouldn't get messed up.

Kimberly confided, "I like to learn about sports. I sorta need help with spelling. I like sports so much—baseball, swimming, soccer, basketball, and I like dinosaurs."

When Chris took his turn he explained, "Building is my life!"

Kimberly confessed that she just wished she could be on a basketball team. She even had a dream about it.

Soothing Kayla

As the children took turns sharing on the carpet, Kayla's mom was losing patience. She had to get the baby home; he was hungry. But Kayla was beyond reason. She sobbed that she didn't want her mom to leave. Talking seemed to make this situation worse. Her mother needed to go and Kayla needed to get on with school.

As the extra person in the room that morning, I volunteered to take Kayla outside to walk around the school while her mother and baby brother left by the other door. Kayla cried brokenheartedly for a few more minutes. She fell to the ground. "I want my mom!!" I soothed her and continued to walk to try to distract her. In a few minutes she was calmer but not ready to go back into the building. I assured her that we did not have to go in yet. This building was a long way around. As we reached the front, I suggested going inside for a drink of water. She agreed and then we toured the school. Finally, we walked back outside and then around to the door near her room. She went in and sat on the edge of the circle. I sat near her for comfort. She had made her entrance and now seemed ready to join the class. Patience with Kayla and her problems the first day might well have set the tone for her whole year.

Louise's Reflections

Usually, I find that it works to distract a worried child with a job to do after saying goodbye to the parent. This depends on the cooperation of the parents. I have never had a child who didn't calm down fairly quickly when the parent left. The job can be as simple as asking the child to take a book and put it on the cabinet on the other side of the room. It depends on how much distress the child is in. For a very upset child, I might hand her a cup and say, "Would you get a cup of water and pour it in the frog's pond in the terrarium?" Lots of jobs can be distracting to a child who doesn't want to face a new group. It helps to refocus their thinking from leaving Mama to a new task. "Would you please go and stir the paint pots on the easel?" "Would you please go help Jim take that mat outside and shake it?" These are some of the many tasks I used to distract a child.

Learning About Lines

Kayla and I had missed the brief trip to the cafeteria. The class was now discussing how to make a line to go the lunchroom. As with so many school things, Louise believed that establishing clear systems by discussing and clarifying expectations would produce good, sensible behavior. She made notes on the board as children made suggestions. She asked, "Why do we need lines? Why don't we all go out the door at the same time?"

The children decided that a line was a quick way to go somewhere. They talked about how there are lines many places, like Taco Bell or A & P. They discussed the importance of going quietly so other people would not be disturbed.

Louise knew that even concepts like quiet needed clarifying for children. "What does quiet mean?" queried Louise. "Who can give me an example?"

One child suggested putting a finger up to your mouth.

"Aren't you old enough to be quiet without a finger over your mouth?"

Jax demonstrated sitting very still with his mouth closed firmly.

Someone said "Hands by your side."

"What else do you need to remember when making a line?"

"Don't push!" said another.

"How can you push if your hands are by your sides?"

"Stomach" was the ready answer.

Just talking about what to do was not enough. Seeing helped. Role-playing is a powerful tool for helping children understand the reason for classroom expectations. Although role-playing and discussion take time at the beginning of the year, much time will be saved later in the year when children know how to behave and choose to do so because they were involved in the process of developing the expectations. Three children were asked to demonstrate leaving and not leaving a space in line. With no spaces, children could have collisions. Kimberly enthusiastically demonstrated a collision. The children hadn't really defined quiet yet, but they would as time went by. The other elements of creating a good line would in fact create a quiet class trip down the hall.

"Can you think of anything else?" asked the teacher.

"Walk," replied the student.

"Who can show us how to walk? What does almost running look like? Where could you run?" Each piece of the trip down the hall was discussed and acted out.

Someone said, "Don't cut."

"We need to talk about that," Louise replied. "In some classes, it's okay to let someone in front of you. Do you want to allow passing or not passing? We can vote on it. Think about it and decide the way you like it."

Decision Making

The children solemnly voted. Six were in favor of passing and seventeen voted not to pass. "How many people do we have in class today?" Twenty-three children were in attendance. Voting gives real-life purpose for understanding numbers and establishes the beginnings of the democratic process in the classroom.

Another child suggested that the class walk on the right so that other classes could get by.

"Can you think of any other place where people have to stay on the right?" Louise mused.

"On a road."

"Actually, you are learning how to drive a car when you walk up and down the hall."

"One Person Can Talk at a Time"

As the discussion continued, one boy began to talk to his neighbor. Louise quietly stopped the child who had the floor. "I can't hear. Someone's talking. We'll wait until they are finished."

The child who was interrupting explained that he was just telling his friend something.

Louise reassured him, "It's okay, we stop and take turns talking. We're waiting until you finish. If two people are talking at one time, we can't hear what they are saying." Her tone was gentle and the reminder nonthreatening, but the importance of courteous listening was underscored.

Louise moved the discussion back to the issue of walking to the lunch room. "We're leaving something out. What's missing?" Seeing puzzled looks, Louise asked, "Have you ever seen someone going down the road looking out the back window?"

Someone replied in excitement, "My mom!"

That was not exactly what Louise had in mind. She clarified by talking about three girls in line ready to come back from the cafeteria, facing in the wrong direction, and getting left behind.

At this point in the class discussion, a little girl raised her hand, "I like the way you pay attention to us. You're like another mother." The child really appreciated the care and respect for children Louise used in explaining what needed to be done.

One child who wanted to finish the discussion asked to do something else. This exciting classroom full of interesting things called out "Play with me" to her. But the centers or learning areas were closed until children were able to discuss how to work in them.

Lunchroom Expectations and Appropriate Voices

The real lunchtime would be soon. The class continued to discuss what to do on the way to and at lunch. Lunchrooms are real challenges for teachers to manage, unless the children know what the appropriate behaviors are for eating in a cafeteria. Louise's children had to be taught about acceptable behaviors and discuss them. Basically, they needed to learn how to behave in public. The children visited the lunchroom earlier in the morning, and before lunch, Louise decided that they needed to discuss what happened during that visit. When the children were in the lunchroom earlier, Kimberly had asked if she could go and talk to her best friend. Louise had told her "No." Louise asked the group, "What are some other ways Kimberly could have said 'hello' to her friend?"

The children eagerly demonstrated appropriate waves. "What else could she give her friend?" "A smile" was the ready reply.

They talked about the use of "tiny little voices" and talking to the people at the table where you are sitting. So often in schools, children are told to "be quiet and keep it down in the lunchroom" without real discussion of what that means and why it is important.

A little boy remembered with panic that he forgot to get his lunch money. Learning responsibility would be a major focus in this class later, but on the first day, the reply was "That's okay. You'll bring it tomorrow."

Ella's Jobs

As the discussion continued, Ella was very busy. She did many little jobs that would help the room run smoothly. She put the children's numbers out in the coat closet in the hall so that each child would have his or her own place for book bags and coats. She put names and numbers on the children's trays. The teachers wrote the children's names clearly to serve as models for use in later work, when other children read and copied names of their classmates.

A Tour of the Room

The children had been sitting a long time. After reviewing a few more expectations about chewing with your mouth closed, and not putting elbows on the table, Louise told the assembled children, "I know you are getting tired. This is what we're going to do, take a quiet tour around the room."

Most of the children got up, eager to see the room, but Sonya was feeling resistant. "I want to play."

Louise explained, "You need to stand up and listen and learn to use the things correctly. But you have a choice, you can stay here and rest." She told the other children, "When the other children are using the centers she won't be able to use them, since she won't know how to use them." Sonya chose to stay where she was.

> **Louise's Reflections**
>
> I assumed that she might join us when she saw what we were doing. If she hadn't, she would've gotten private instruction from me or Ella when the other children began to use the areas. I saw no point in getting into a power struggle with Sonya. I always avoided power struggles because I knew that no one would win. When I gave choices, a power struggle was avoided.

Games Area With that, Louise began to talk about the games. Everyone, except Sonya, stood quietly listening while Louise showed the games and the special places on the shelves for their boxes. In the library area that surrounded the group meeting area, the books were organized into categories with little cards dividing them. The puppet center had puppets available on pegs behind the theater and the cupboard behind the stage had big trays full of things to use for dress up and for plays.

The children followed Louise around the room looking at the child-safe paper cutter, the places for project work, all the science books, the series books, and the math materials. Everything was out and available for student use. The aim was for children to be independent and able to gather the materials they needed for their work.

Cooking Center Louise showed them that the cooking center had a mid-size refrigerator, a pegboard with labeled cooking tools, a toaster oven, cookbooks, a sink, and plenty of promise. She told them that the table is used for working in the morning and for cooking in the afternoon. She explained that cooking, sewing, and carpentry had real tools that could hurt them so the many rules that apply to them must be discussed before the centers could open. The children were full of anticipation.

Louise told the children a bit about the cooking center (see Figure 2–1). "We'll have a calendar and you'll sign up. On pretty days we'll go outside to sell what we make. Here's a chef's hat to keep your hair out of everything. Here are the can openers and knives."

Figure 2–1.   *The cooking center.*

"Are they very sharp?" inquired a cautious soul.

"If it is very sharp, we'd like for an adult to be there when you use them. You can use the dinner knives [which are not sharp] without an adult nearby. We have a form where you will write your recipes."

The children were crowded close together and two girls became angry. Louise quickly surveyed the situation and helped the two girls realize that the bumping was accidental. The problem was solved with a "sorry" from Kimberly who still looked a bit angry.

Art Area   The group moved on to the art area "where you construct and make stuff." Kayla was still on the periphery of the group. Sonya had sidled over near the discussion but was not quite part of it, although she did appear to be listening.

Bathroom   Next on the tour was a very important room. The bathroom just off the classroom only had one toilet in it. "How many people need to use the bathroom at once?" The children quickly agreed that one at a time made sense. Louise pointed out numbered cloths hanging on clothespins mounted on the wall on a long, narrow wooden board. "These will be assigned to each of you. It will be your responsibility to use it to help clean the classroom, wash it out, wring it out, and put it back in the proper place."

Louise's Reflections

In schools where we didn't have a bathroom in the classroom, I created systems so that the children could come and go independently. For younger children, I usually made signs to wear around their necks. Older children preferred hall passes made of wood. The rule was one child out of the room at a time unless it was a dire emergency (in which case the child with the emergency needed to talk to the teacher). I talked to the children in large group to set the parameters for how the passes where to be used. If a child didn't follow the parameters, that child would require a person to go with him. Most kids preferred being independent and going on their own. To me, it has always seemed strange to expect that twenty-four children would need to use the bathroom at the same time.

Sand   The large sand table was near the bathroom. The children considered things to remember when working in sand. "Sand needs to stay in its place. If you spill it, what do you do? We have to take care of the sand so that it doesn't disappear." Children also needed to think about how to care for the sand. The teacher used questions to help the children develop necessary expectations for the sand. "How would you use the tubs? What would happen if you scatter the sand outside the sandbox? Before you walk away from the sand table, what should you do?" The children were quick to respond, their faces vivid with anticipation.

Logistics   How many people can each center hold? The answer to this question was determined by the space, chairs, and number of sides. At the sand area the children guessed six, eight, or four people. Louise pointed out the two long sides of the sand box. Many years of experience had made her aware of space limits and the kinds of consequences that occur when too many children work in too small a space.

The Rest of the Day

After Lunch   At lunch everyone did well following the expectations they had established that morning. They all wanted to see their guidelines carried out successfully. The morning's planning seemed to have worked. At various times throughout the year, the expectations would need to be reviewed by the children.

Story Sharing   After lunch every day would be quiet time for story sharing. Today, Louise had chosen *My Great Aunt Arizona* by Gloria Houston for a read aloud. This beautifully illustrated story has North Carolina mountain roots and highlights the excitement of school and reading.

At the end of the story, Arizona, a school teacher, had taught about far-away places for thirty-two years but she had visited those places only in her mind. Louise shared her emotional reaction to the story. Ella had to finish reading the book because it was so sad, and Louise left the circle to regain composure and wipe her eyes.

Kayla, the child who had begun the day with tears, got up to see what had happened to her teacher. I was standing near the edge of the circle taking notes. I whispered to Kayla, "Mrs. Burrell really needs a hug. The book made her sad."

Kayla gave Louise a heartfelt hug, while Louise told her that grown-ups cry, too. Louise told Kayla that her hug helped but she needed another—and that she would probably need a hug in the morning also. Kayla looked more relaxed and at peace than she had all day. Hugs usually help the hugger as well as the huggee!

Louise's Reflections

I think that it is important for teachers to show all kinds of feelings: caring, empathy, and perhaps even frustration at themselves. The children needed to see how I handled frustration as well as disappointment. For instance, when I lost my glasses, the children saw my aggravation with myself. They helped me make plans to keep track of my glasses. On the other hand, I believe that a teacher should never show a child that she feels anger, uses sarcasm, or has an air of superiority toward children. A child needs to know that while you may not approve of everything he has done, you still like and care for him. This caring is reflected in your interactions with the child and in problem solving.

After the story, the children and Louise continued the room tour by discussing the blocks, Legos, other building materials, social studies books, the paper center, the display of bones, and the publishing center.

Kayla moved over to Mrs. Ensley, "What's her name again?"

"Mrs. Burrell."

Getting Help

The children were ready to get to work. Louise knew that there were many more things that they needed to know. Much retraining of typical school procedures was necessary for this classroom. "What do you do when you need help?" Practically in unison, the children replied, "Raise your hand."

"That's one way, but not exactly the answer I'm looking for."

"Ask a teacher."

"No."

"Ask a friend."

The children needed to know that help comes from *many* people, not just a teacher. This understanding was a start toward moving responsibility from the exclusive control of the teachers to the children themselves. If the children couldn't get answers from friends then, of course, they could go to the teachers. However, Louise wanted to challenge the assumption that the teacher is the primary source of information. This process of learning how to give help started on day one and would continue throughout the year. The children would also need to learn how to give help.

Communications

Numbered mailboxes gave the children another way to communicate among themselves and another reason to read and write. Children were encouraged to write notes and cards for their peers. Often they used the mailboxes to convey useful information to each other or their teachers. They had to read carefully to put mail in the correct slots.

The paper center was full of all different kinds of paper. There was a large bookshelf that held various types of large paper—some for the easel, some lined, some colored, and blank white paper. The little shelves housed various smaller sizes of lined and unlined paper for writing as well as small colored construction paper, index cards, and colored card stock. "What do you need to remember?" asked Louise.

"Not to waste it."

"Right, we care about the trees and the earth."

Great Expectations—Listening and Following Directions

By now, the children and teacher had made a circle around the room and had done the preliminary look at what would be available. They were back in the group area and anxious to get started. Yet there were more things that had to be taken care of. Louise said that they needed more instructions. Two boys had not seated themselves yet. Louise watched them quietly until they sat down. She began to talk about the tray of working tools and the supplies many of the children had brought to school in response to a before-school letter. When she began the instructions about where to put these materials, most of the children jumped up to get their book bags. They had not listened to the rest of the instructions.

"Let's just let them go if they know what to do."

As the children returned, she admonished very quietly and firmly, "You have to learn to listen and follow directions."

Those children who stayed seated whispered to the ones who jumped up, "Put it back, put it back."

Louise was waiting until all were ready. "Do you know how much time we just lost?" she asked when the group settled down. "You only heard the first part. Listen until the person who's doing the talking does what . . . ?" she paused.

"Finishes!" answered the children.

Going Home

On the first day, the class stopped a little early in order for the children to learn the system for dismissal. The children lined up according to their assigned buses. Louise asked them to look at the other children on their bus. They needed to know who was in their group so that they could watch out for each other like sisters and brothers would do. Throughout the year, the children made sure that everyone was on the bus. When problems arose on the bus, they were there to help each other.

First Day's Lessons

Today, on the first day of school, the children had been in awe of all that filled the room. At the beginning of the day they hesitated, wondering what would be expected of them, because this class looked so different from classrooms they had been in before. The difference in the room was by design; this room had been created to *empower* children.

Louise's Reflections

My classroom was designed to provide opportunities for children to be curious and wonder and to provide places for them to bump up against problems. The children had so much to learn. They'd learn to solve problems together in a whole class council, in small groups, and individually. My children would learn that they had control over themselves and their environment. Ultimately, they'd take responsibility for taking care of the room, themselves, their learning, and each other.

This ability to control themselves and their environment would be empowering and would foster the children's intrinsic motivation. All of these things began on the first day of school and set the tone for the year.

Things to Remember During the First Days

Following are some things to remember during the first days of school. These things do not occur necessarily in the order listed here. They happen simultaneously and recursively. All are essential to the creation of community in any classroom at all levels.

The children need to feel comfortable and at ease.

In this account of the first day, notice how the assistant's greeting drew the children into the room. Rather than having to take seats and be quiet immediately, the children were able to walk around and look at the exciting possibilities and materials. They had a chance to greet friends and re-establish relationships with former classmates. Especially on this first day, they needed time to get to know each other and their teachers in informal and personal ways. The tone needs to be happy and relaxed.

Louise's Reflections

Some teachers advise, "Don't smile before Christmas." This is phooey. Children need to feel welcomed, wanted, loved, and competent. Also, they need assigned places to put their personal belongings and their working materials, so that they feel a sense of security, feel that they are a part of the room, and that they have their own special spaces. They also need to become immediately involved in setting the expectations that will govern the room.

All children need to feel comfortable and at ease in a new classroom. For example, an older child who comes in and sits, who speaks only when spoken to, who worries about being wrong and not being able to do what is asked is an uncomfortable child—a lonely child. Upper-grade children, even more than primary children, need their peers to like and accept them. They want to feel part of the new group. Activities that promote comfort are vital for the developing community; without them school can be a scary place. Children need an atmosphere where they are free to express their opinions and have those opinions honored. They need to make choices and decisions in order to feel in control of their lives.

Academic work does not need to begin for several days until the children have been introduced to the room and each other.

The teacher needs a chance to get to know the children, to see them and hear them in nonthreatening situations. Some children come into school frightened and need a period of comfortable adjustment so that they can feel ready for the academics. There will be plenty of time later for academics. By the second or third day, writing about something like families or pets will be assigned. Whatever each person does on these safe open-ended writing tasks will be accepted.

Make modifications as needed, as the children and teacher evaluate the room and see changes that need to be made in the environment.

The reorganization in the group meeting area that was made before the group sharing began took only a few minutes, but it signaled to the children that their needs and comfort were important to their teachers. During the first days of school, teachers and children will find many places in the environment that need to be rearranged and modified. Necessary changes to the environment need to happen as soon as the need arises.

Teachers and students need to examine the room together to be sure it is working for them. The environment creates systems that can help or hinder the developing community. A harmonious community is hard to achieve when the teacher alone makes decisions about room arrangement, leaving the children without a voice. Teachers who dictate often must resort to loud voices, constant reminders, and prodding in efforts to control the room and the students. The beginning of the school year is an ideal time for teacher and students working together to begin assessing their needs in relationship to the environment.

Begin the vital work of creating community by sharing personal information.

The initial sharing conversation serves many purposes. One is to get the children talking. They are taking turns and the teacher notices some are more eager than others. Not all of them share in this first discussion. Later, the children are asked to introduce themselves by sharing more about their summer experiences. When the teacher gets ready to call on them, she calls on those who shared freely in this first conversation. These confident, talkative children are models for the quieter children. They model both topics of conversation and being comfortable in speaking in front of the large group. Sharing personal information is comfortable for most children. Talking about what is important to them and things they know about helps them feel part of the group and helps lay the foundation for expressing themselves in writing.

Begin the conversations about the habits the children need to learn in order to function in the room and the school.

In working with the children to consider what a line is and how to make a good line, Louise began the process of helping the children develop self-control. Not talking in the hall showed respect and consideration for the other people in the building. Crucial words like self-control were introduced on the first day of school in a purposeful context. These concepts would be taught over and over throughout the school year. Children needed to learn to control all parts of their bodies: their hands, their eyes, their ears, their mouths, their feet, and arms. They needed to be aware that they are individually in control of themselves. Each person had to decide to make wise choices and to exercise self-control. Nobody could make another person talk or listen or think or react. Each person was responsible for each of his or her actions.

The children would not instantly become successful from this beginning discussion of how to walk in line. Time after time they would need to be reminded; they would need to discuss the issues again and role-play them. Later in the year (after the introduction of concepts about quality), quality indicators for walking in a line would be established. Sometimes as the children were working on self-control, the teacher would need to talk to an individual, and sometimes to the whole group. This process of discussion took more time than simply insisting on obedience and compliance, but the end result was that children would grow into responsible adults who would be in charge of themselves. If every teacher worked on self-control every year, what a better world we would have! Freedom only works well when people learn to take responsibility.

Also, the time spent at the beginning of the year on self-control builds a strong foundation for a year of learning. If the foundation is weak, much time is wasted later when teachers must admonish children daily. Techniques like reprimanding children or writing their names on the board do not usually improve behavior in the long run. Children need to consider the "whys" of behaving in appropriate ways in the classroom. When they want to be part of the community and want the community to run smoothly, then and only then will they try to develop self-control. Children who learn to control their behavior work harder and smarter.

In this class, the teacher was not the boss or the police officer out to catch the unwary but a guide to help children move through the school experience with success. As the adult in the classroom and the teacher, she was firmly in charge and the children knew this. At the beginning of the year, her body language communicated as much as her words did. Standing near a child, looking a child in the eye, or gently touching a child on the shoulder were powerful nonverbal ways of showing the children that she was in charge and cared for them. Louise wanted to share power with the children in the class. The more she could give control over to the children and could teach them to control themselves, the more independent and responsible they would become.

These discussions of how to behave began the process of empowering the children. Empowering children would lead to their intrinsic motivation.

Establish expectations for behavior as they tour the room and consider how each area will be used.

The centers were powerful motivators for getting the children's cooperation. From long experience and much trial and error, Louise knew many of the things that the children needed to do and not do in each area. However, she wanted the guidelines to come from the children. Children are invested in following guidelines that they help develop. Their discussions on expectations empowered the children and fostered the developing community. At the heart of every community are shared expectations.

The room was designed to encourage the children to make choices and wise decisions. The room was also designed so that children would encounter problems and make mistakes. If everything were to go smoothly all the time no one would have to stop and consider solutions to problems. The room is truly part of the thinking curriculum.

Louise's Reflections

I believe that people learn when they make mistakes, reflect on them, and then work to improve. My children would soon learn that in this class "mistakes are stepping stones to learning." This meant that everyone makes mistakes and mistakes are not times for blame and recriminations. Mistakes are opportunities to think about what has happened and figure out better strategies for the future.

Some centers such as woodworking, sewing, and cooking would not open until the children had learned to use many of the other materials in the room independently. Having to wait for some special centers made developing self-control even more important for the children. They wanted to cook, sew, and do woodworking, and they were willing to make efforts at being self-controlled.

Habits and expectations need to be established at the beginning of the year in any grade level. People of all ages need to know what is expected of them—especially in new situations. In addition, people who feel that they helped develop and make decisions about the expectations are more likely to abide by those expectations. People must know the reasons behind the expectations and regulations they live by. Research is clear that teachers who spend time on these kinds of discussions at the beginning of the year, have classes that run smoothly with less disruption later in the year.

Tell and read aloud stories to begin teaching concepts like empathy, respect for individual differences, worth of their own heritage, and responsibility.

Sharing literature and stories is appropriate at all age levels. Good stories touch people's souls and sharing stories bonds people into communities. Stories form vital parts of the history of groups. Careful selection of read alouds can enrich the caring curriculum as well as teach academic goals. Discussions around the books read or stories told work on reading comprehension while linking people's histories together in meaningful ways.

Key Components: What Children Need from the First Day

Comfort, conversation, empowerment, expectations, and sharing are vital elements in the beginning of a school community. Paying attention to these things creates a strong foundation for building academics. All children, even the toughest ones who bring with them years of pain and defenses, have soft, gentle cores. Over the years they have added layers of defenses for self-protection. Children with too many protective layers are not ready to learn. Before they can learn academics, they need time to learn to trust, to feel like somebody cares, and to begin to learn that they are important. The first day of school is the first opportunity the teacher has to diffuse some of their negative expectations.

At the end of the first day, we hope each child going out the door thinks these thoughts:

- My teacher listened to me. She likes me.
- I got to share how I think we should do some things.
- The other children listened to me.
- My teacher seemed real—she makes mistakes and has feelings.
- I can't wait until tomorrow—I know where I want to work.
- I know just what I want to share tomorrow.

Louise's Reflections

If children leave the first day with these thoughts in their heads, I know that their fear and stress can begin to dissolve and their desire to do, achieve, and succeed can take hold. In the upcoming days when the children come through the door to the class, I'll see smiles, sparkling eyes, hear hurrying feet, eager conversations, and joyous laughter. I'll greet children each morning who are excited and glad to be in school.

3

The First Weeks of School:
Getting Down to Work

Education is not the filling of the pail, but the lighting of the fire.
—W. B. YEATS

On the second day of school, the teachers began the process of creating a predictable daily schedule that guides them throughout the year. The rituals and routines of a school day create community. During the first weeks of school, children need to be involved in developing the schedules, systems, and expectations that will guide them throughout the year.

The children were still more interested in all the enticing materials in the room than in talking "on the carpet." After sharing time on Friday morning, the second day of school, the children wanted to know, "When do we get to play?"

Louise was not quite ready; the room tour on the first day of school was just an introduction. The children needed to understand that they would work as well as play in the learning areas. "We have to learn how to use the areas. Who can tell me some things to remember about the woodworking area?" They began by discussing woodworking and then mentally moved through the room talking about other areas. This time, the children were reviewing the previous lesson by telling the teacher how to use the areas. She wanted the children to learn that the materials in the room were working tools, not just toys for play.

Second Day Assignments

After the large group discussion on centers, Louise gave each child a blank book. These were teacher-made, spiral-bound books made from blank ditto paper. Each book had a line guide in a pocket in the back. The line guide could be placed under any sheet of paper to give children lines to write on when needed. This first book, called "Investigations," was only one of many to come later in the year. This book was for math, science, social studies, health, goal setting, and writing. Most assignments required the children to integrate knowledge from several disciplines.

Part of the first assignment for the Investigations book was to create a cover design for the book. The first assignments were simple and open-ended. Some of the first assignments were designed to get the children working in the centers and to see the room as a resource. On the second day, in addition to designing covers for their Investigations books, the children were to find work to do somewhere in the room, and make a record to show what they did. Louise explained, "You can record it by drawing a picture, making a chart or graph, or just writing what you do. You will share this after lunch in big group." This open assignment allowed the children to investigate, plan, record, and make choices and decisions.

Louise needed to assess their understanding of their trip around the class on the first day of school as well as their class discussion. She wanted to see if the children knew how to use the materials and could control their bodies as they moved around the room.

Integrated Work Time

When the large group meeting was over, Louise sent them off to explore. She said, "You may go to work." The children left the large group area and moved all around the room. They chose where they wanted to work. It was their choice how long they stayed in each area. The areas were simply working spaces full of tools, resources, and materials.

Since the assignment was to find work somewhere in the room and record what they did, the children began working in the various areas. They were, Louise noted, "a bit wild, hurrying with loud voices." She explained to me that this was to be expected. The children had not yet established the quality indicators for communication. Some children explored materials in the dramatic play area. One child made a clay dolphin. Another child made a rectangular solid from blocks. All over the room, the children found materials and created their own meanings.

None of these centers or learning areas were required and none had time limitations imposed on them. The areas contained the raw materials and tools that the children needed to do their work. The materials in the learning areas were chosen also for their attractiveness to children and to capture children's attention. During the working period, both Louise and Ella moved among the children to guide their work and behavior and encourage explorations. Some children had to be reminded of quiet voices; others needed to be encouraged to try things. Some children seemed reluctant to take risks and investigate the materials. They needed assurance to begin to feel comfortable in the room.

Initial Assessments

As the children worked in the different learning areas, Louise watched and assessed them both academically and socially. During this time the children were reading, writing, and communicating orally. While she was concerned with their academic skills and strategies, she was also aware that a child's level of confidence might well determine his or her likelihood of using those skills and strategies effectively. The choice and use of centers or learning areas fell along both academic and confidence lines. More mature children chose the books to read while others worked with the clay. Low self-esteem and fear of failure often deterred children from trying the more academic tasks. Gradually, over a period of time, permission to work on doable tasks would help those children who had not experienced school success before develop confidence in their abilities to "handle school."

Individual Assessment Time

Children's work time was important teacher time. Teachers need time to observe children and to assess their growing understanding. The teachers were careful to build in time during the integrated work period to watch and listen to children. Throughout the year during the integrated work time, the teacher and her assistant worked with children individually or in small groups by giving whatever academic help was needed. One of the reasons this worked was because the teachers were teaching the children how to be independent. Children were encouraged to work hard and try to solve problems themselves. They were often able to take care of their own problems because they were taught how to give and get help from each other.

Getting to Know the Children

A teacher needs to see where each child is so she can facilitate their growth both academically and socially. Work time was a perfect opportunity for Louise to assess children. Louise had enormous faith in the potential of all the children in her class. She saw them realistically and individually but also held a shining picture in her mind of what each child could be and do. The children felt the power of this belief. When I first started going to her room, I remember the principal telling me that what impressed him about Louise was she could tell him about the reading levels of all the children in her class. I agreed that she did quickly assess each child's reading level and each child's understanding of key concept in mathematics and science. And even more important to me was the way she connected to the soul of each child and grew to understand each heart. This understanding is the key to authentic teaching.

Lunch Time

Lunch time comes early in many elementary schools, whether people are hungry or not. Lunch in the cafeteria was a learning time for the children in Louise's class. Children learned to serve themselves, to converse quietly with friends at their table, and to use good manners in eating.

Story Time

After lunch, the children and teacher gathered back in the group area to share a book. This was generally the teacher's time to read a book to the whole group. Reading aloud is a vital part of the reading program at any grade level. Before children want to become readers, they must enjoy stories and feel the power of a good book. They need to see a teacher model reading aloud with expression and feeling. The teacher should ask questions to assess and develop children's comprehension. Their vocabularies grow when new words are heard in context and then discussed. Discussing good stories and reviewing the chapters that were read the day before helps children identify the elements of story like plot and character in nonthreatening comfortable ways. Listening to stories, especially chapter books, develops the reading habit and helps children learn that reading can be done over time—some of the best books are read over several weeks. Finally, good stories help children develop empathy and understanding for people in other situations.

Sharing Time

When story time was over, the children went and got their work from the morning to share with the group. This sharing was a first step toward accountability. As children told what they had made and done, they gave each other ideas about other possibilities. The teachers kept track of who had shared to

Figure 3–1. *Sharing time.*

be sure that all children had equal turns. Sharing with the group lent meaning and seriousness to their self-chosen activities. Later in the year this time was used for project or dramatic presentations. Sharing time was used flexibly throughout the year (see Figure 3–1).

Kayla Thrives

The day flowed easily from large group, to individual work, to sharing work. Later I saw the fruits of the comfortable community that was being developed when I saw Kayla again. I was relieved to hear that after her shaky beginning on the first day, Kayla had adjusted quickly. She rode the bus to school and had a part in the impromptu play the children planned based on the book read the previous day. Experiencing the first day gave her a predictable frame for making sense of the schedule of the room and gave her comfort. Also, the accepting attitude that greeted her after her outburst allowed her to slip smoothly, without embarrassment, into the emerging community. The children learned that being sad is a part of life and that if other people care, the sadness may pass.

Building Community Through Drama

After story time and sharing I watched the children put on an informal play based on *My Great Aunt Arizona*. They used the dress up materials and had a narrator. Drama was often a way for the children to make some concept personally meaningful. Lots of kids were in the play. Some, who were shy on the first day, acted their parts with flourish the second day. Expectations of unpressured participation were set. As the year continued, many children who began shy and uncomfortable emerged as leaders with plenty to say.

For the play, Karen got up to read *My Great Aunt Arizona* while the others acted it out. "I'm going to read it. I'm not a very good reader," she confided to Louise.

Louise commented to me later, "She needs confidence building." She also noted that Chris, "a beautiful little boy," needed to develop self-control of his body, especially in relation to the other twenty-four children. He was an impulsive child who blurted out comments and interrupted his peers and his teachers. He often bumped into the other children and bothered them. Each child was special. Each child had his or her strengths and areas that needed work. All of them would learn about continuous improvement.

A Typical Daily Schedule

One morning in early September, Louise said to the children, "Let's work out our schedule for each day. First we have to start with the things we have to do that have already been scheduled. Could you name some of these for me?"

The children began with lunchtime and remembered that art, music, and P.E. had special times assigned. They understood that neither they nor Louise had control over the times for these out-of-class activities.

Then Louise said, "We need to make a chart to organize our time." She asked for suggestions for a title.

The children's suggestions ranged from "My Schedule," "Our Daily Schedule," "Work Time," to "Our Work." They voted and decided to call the chart, "Our Daily Schedule."

Louise's Reflections

In doing this, I was teaching the children the beginning steps of making one kind of chart. Having a daily schedule is important so that the children can plan and organize their time and work. When they help make the schedule chart, then they can read it and use it. The chart is also a wonderful reason to learn to tell time.

On the board, Louise listed all the things the children mentioned that they needed to do each day. She included the times that had already been established. The children and Louise then talked about when activities such as sharing, reflections, work time, and cleanup could occur. As these things were mentioned, they talked about what each entailed. Later, Ella transferred what had been written on the board to a chart that was posted in the room. A copy was later put into the children's planning books.

The first two columns on the following chart were similar to the chart that was used by the children. The comments in the third column briefly describe what each activity entails. Following the schedule listed below is an explanation of each period of the day in some detail.

Our Daily Schedule

Time	Activity	Comments
8:00–8:45	Sharing time	The children are in charge of the rituals to begin the day.
8:45–9:30	Teacher time	Teacher provides review, instruction, and directions for work to whole class.
9:30–Lunch (11:20 or so)	Integrated work time	Children work in learning areas (centers) to complete givens and choose activities while teachers work as needed with individuals or groups. Teacher may pull the children back to large group if necessary at any time.
11:20–11:45	Lunch	
11:45–12:30	Reading	Reading includes story time, DEAR (Drop Everything and Read) time, and small group reading. Some days a sharing time was scheduled before the children went back to work.
12:30–2:15	Integrated work time	Children return to work unless there is a presentation scheduled, work sharing period, or a special activity outside the classroom.
2:15–2:30	Cleanup	Each child has chosen an area to clean.
2:30–3:00	Reflections and final sharing time	The day ends with writing in journals for reflection and more large group meeting.

In this process of discussing time schedules, the children began developing independence, responsibility, dependability, and assuming ownership of their classroom community. While the general outline of group time and work time remained constant year after year, the daily schedule was subject to change each day depending on the needs of the children. Teachers who embrace the importance of this process (and are willing to spend the necessary time in conversations with their children at the beginning of the year) are rewarded by children who know how to live and learn cooperatively.

Sharing Time

From 8:00 to 8:45, the first period of the day was called sharing time. On the first day or two of school, sharing was led by Louise; however, she quickly turned the task of leading the sharing period over to the children. Louise's system of keeping track of turns was based on a simple chart with children's names under each day of the week called the Sharing Chart. During the first few days of school, Louise observed which children seemed most confident and comfortable in front of the class. These children were put at the beginning of the list as models for the other children. The rest of the children were placed randomly on the chart. The chart then had five columns and five or six rows.

On the first Monday the chart was used, Jax was the leader. The following week, Tommy was the leader on Monday, and so forth. Once the system was up and running the day's leader rotated *down* the column for that day. For example, if Kayla was absent on a Monday, the child below her on the chart, Meg, took her turn. Each day's children kept track of whose turn it was on that day. The children quickly understood the progression from day to day and week to week. Keeping track was easy; the children always knew who was next. Children did not want to be absent or come in late and miss their turn. An absence meant that the person in the row below the absent leader would become leader for that day. For example, when Sonya was sick, then Sarah took her turn. Sonya would have to wait for the rotation to come back to her.

Sharing Chart

Monday	Tuesday	Wednesday	Thursday	Friday
Jax	Kimberly	Alice	Jason	Frank
Tommy	Chris	Sonya	Timmy	Marc
Kayla	Tim	Sarah	Sam	Dan
Meg	Kate	Molly	Jake	Will
Dylan	Clyde	Doris	Beth	David

Louise always started the use of the sharing chart on a Monday, usually at the beginning of the second week of school. She talked about the chart on Friday so that Monday's leader would be prepared with something to read and share.

Sharing time was run by the children and included a number of rituals and routines that marked the beginning of each school day. Rituals are a vital part of creating community. Louise began some of the rituals and the children quickly created others. The children met "on the carpet" at the front of the room in the group meeting area. The leader sat on the bench under the white board and the other children sat on the floor in front of the leader. The first order of business was sharing. In the beginning, each child in the class could share one thing. But by the fourth day, sharing time took too long and the children were feeling the need for more work time. They met as a group and decided how long they could afford to spend together. They also decided how much time the teacher should have to talk. Later in the year when the children had many more things to be done during the day, they decided to limit turns to share to only the children of the day. Throughout the year, special permission was always granted for special events such as the birth of a new baby brother or sister.

The year began with personal sharing, which helped the children become acquainted and helped each child understand and respect the differences in family experiences. Some children brought in things from home and others just shared their experiences. They began to realize that other people's families might be different from their own and that the differences are okay. This was a wonderful time for the children to develop leadership skills and confidence in speaking to a large group.

While this sharing was going on, Louise worked unobtrusively in the background. She wanted the children to feel that this was truly their time. But at the same time, she listened carefully. If a child shared something that might be upsetting or difficult for the others to understand, she would slip back into the group and "smooth the waters." For example, a few years ago one child began to tell about how his father had just gone to prison. The child did not explain why his dad was in prison. Louise went up quickly and sat down beside him, hugged him, and said, "I'm really sorry to hear that." To the group she added, "Sometimes we do things without thinking and the consequences are not good. This year we'll be working on learning to think about what we do before we do it." She was very careful with what she said because she knew her words would affect the little child whose father was in prison as well as the other children. She had to let all the children know that we bear the consequences of our actions, but she did not want the other children to form negative opinions of the child whose father was in prison. She told the children a story about a boy who unknowingly got involved with the wrong group of people and got in trouble. Her calm acceptance of the child and his situation showed the other children how to express caring for a friend in need.

Leader of the Day

The sharing time was organized by the first part of a flowchart called Leader of the Day that was developed with the children on the second day of school.

Leader of the Day

Conducts sharing

Conducts game

Shares book

Does calendar

Informs teacher that it is her turn

Reminds others to sign up for small group

Does reading

Gives assistance to peers

Leads line

Delivers messages for teachers

Cleans tables

Holds doors the next day

After the children shared, they always played a group mental math game. Louise had developed a basket that was full of game cards. The game was designed for everyone to be involved at the same time. To participate in the play, all the children had to be alert. The original game came from the state department curriculum materials and Louise expanded it into many versions dealing with all subjects. All she needed for each game was a set of cards with one question and one answer for each child in the room. The children developed a ritual for playing the game. The leader passed out the cards and collected them.

The leader of the day had many responsibilities. After the game, the child shared a book or a special part of a book with the group. The leader prepared the book in advance. The leader selected a book from the class or brought one in from home. The leader was supposed to stick to time limitations, usually ten minutes. However, depending on the needs of the reader, Louise sometimes varied the time. Occasionally, she would have to prompt an overzealous reader with, "Are you almost finished?"

After the sharing, game playing, and reading, the leader did the work with the calendar. He or she had to put up the day of the week, month, then ask questions concerning the calendar such as, "If last Monday was the eleventh then what will next Monday be?" To begin the year, Louise made a card with questions to cue the leader; this card was then changed to increase the level of difficulty. Later the children developed their own questions like, "How do you spell this month?" "How many days in this month?"

The leader of the day's work was not done at the end of sharing time. He or she was the designated helper for those who needed assistance during the day. If the leader was unable to help, then he or she would bring the child to the teacher. Having someone to go with them to the teacher gave confidence to a shy child. The leader was also responsible for such tasks as leading all lines and delivering messages outside the classroom.

Teacher Time

After the calendar, the leader went to the teacher to tell her that it was her turn. At the beginning of the year, Louise used this time to assess the children and to review concepts. Using the board, she might review letters, words, the alphabet, and teach simple lessons on capitalization and rhyming families. She tried to help the children understand things like why we use capitalization or need to pay attention to rhyming words. These were short lessons. Then she might introduce a math concept like the difference between even and odd.

Givens

During the first week of school, Louise used her teacher time to introduce another key concept that would allow the children to use centers for work and play and to manage their time. She wanted to make sure that the children were acquiring the skills and understandings that she knew were needed. She wanted her children to learn the academics but she also wanted to help them work toward responsibility, dependability, and persistence. Her children needed to learn that all these things were "givens" or requirements. Louise's children were learning that at the same time they had choices, they were responsible for completing certain givens.

The children had to learn that along with freedom and fun there were also required expectations. Louise explained, "*Givens* are things that you have to do whether you want to or not. Adults have givens that they must be responsible for." Louise asked the children, "As an adult, if I want to drive a car, what do I need to have?" They eagerly responded, "A driver's license." She continued, "When I am driving, how do I know how fast I can go? What happens if I exceed the speed limit?" Children usually know that adults have to follow rules. The children have heard about speed limits and paying for things in stores. It makes them feel better to realize that even adults have constraints on their freedom. They know that when the givens are met there are many freedoms available in the grown-up world. The classroom is the same way—

when the children participate as good citizens in the community and meet their givens, they have many choices and freedoms.

After establishing a preliminary understanding of the word *givens,* Louise and the children developed a givens chart. Children had to complete their work, be caring, and be safe. Everybody was expected to read every day. Louise explained to the children that just like our bodies need different kinds of food to grow and develop, so do our brains. Brain "foods" include talking, reading, observing, writing, thinking, dreaming, and doing. Givens also included the vital concept of quality. The children were expected to do all their work to the best of their abilities.

Another important given was cleanup. Givens also included the requirement that children would work in all the centers or learning areas. This did not mean that children had to go to each center each day. Louise expected that children would use all the areas over an extended period of time.

Givens

Be safe

Be courteous and caring

Work toward goals and standards

Read

Report cards

Do all your work: recording books, baggie books, projects

Strive for quality

Cleanup

Use *all* the learning areas

Goals and Standards

Louise tied the work the children needed to do to the state curriculum guidelines. These guidelines were also a given. Louise showed the children a copy of the state standard course of study. Their state has a relatively straightforward list of competencies for each discipline. Louise posted a copy of the relevant competencies so the parents could refer to them and know what was expected. With help, the children could see how what they were learning was related to the requirements of the state.

Reading

The children would learn that "givens" in reading included many different types of reading times. The children listened to the leader read aloud each morning and to the teachers during story time after lunch. During quiet reading time (DEAR time), all children read books they selected themselves. They were expected to record what they read in their reading logs.

In the afternoon after the teacher had shared her book and DEAR time, the class was divided into small groups for more book sharing directed by the children. During small group reading time or literature circles, children listened to one child in the group read aloud and then discussed the selection as a group. All centers were closed and each group had a spot in the room where the children would sit in a circle on the floor. The reader was in charge of his or her small group. The groups were formed earlier each day when the children on the sharing chart for the day wrote the titles of their previously self-selected books on a wipe-off chart. The other children read the book titles and signed up as part of a group to hear about one of the books. This process developed high interest in books and enhanced reading comprehension. As the children shared, they often discussed and disagreed about the meanings of stories. Children can enjoy discussing their reading just as much as adults do.

Every afternoon the children selected another book to take home to read independently or with their parents. They took their books home in large plastic bags. These take-home books were called "baggie books." Later in the year when the children worked on projects they often read extensively for information—finding both fiction and nonfiction books that related to their projects.

Report Cards

Report cards were also a given. Louise did not particularly like them, but she was required by the school district to send them home every grading period. She and the children also worked to create their own systems for grading that involved consideration of effort, response to feedback, and progress.

Louise's Reflections

I don't like anything about "traditional" report cards based on letter or number grades. They rank children without taking their effort and progress into consideration. They don't really give useful feedback as to what a child is really doing or needs to work on for improvement. I think that looking at children's work over time and keeping track of their work habits and skill development provides much more important information—both for planning instruction and for communicating with parents. Self-assessment and goal setting by the children is much more valuable than assigning G's, E's, A's, or B's.

Figure 3–2. *Small group book sharing chart and sign-up.*

Cleanup

In a room like Louise's, full of materials and active learning, good systems for cleanup are essential. A teacher could never straighten out all the learning areas and prepare them for the next day by herself. Besides, children only become responsible when they have real and necessary jobs to do. Caring for a classroom is a first step toward caring for the earth.

Very early in the year, the teachers introduced a caring chart. Each learning area in the room was designated a cleanup area and one or two children were assigned responsibility for the area. When the chart was first introduced, the teachers matched jobs with children. Later, job applications were available and the first child who filled out the form correctly with the earliest date got the position.

When Louise called for cleanup, the children would stop working, put their things away, and go to get their cleanup badges. Ella had used a badge-making machine and pictures of the cleanup areas from the chart to make each child a badge to wear. With the badges the teachers could quickly check to see if the children were in their proper areas. All the children had cleaning cloths with their own numbers on them to use for cleaning and dusting areas.

The teacher and children created a flowchart to describe the steps in the cleanup process. The children followed the flowchart and completed their jobs. The children had also developed quality indicators for cleanup. When they finished with their own areas they could only help in another area if the person in charge wanted help. When they finished and the room was ready for the next day, they were expected to evaluate themselves according to the quality indicators. The teacher helped them self-check especially when specific children were off task. The children also evaluated each other and were often very demanding. Sometimes children wrote about cleanup during their reflections.

Quality Cleanup Indicators

Accepts responsibility willingly

Starts to work quickly

Returns objects to proper places

Dusts

Completes own center, then helps others

Completes job in allotted time

Continues to work until room is clean

Reflections and Final Sharing Time

After cleanup, the children took out their planning books, found places to sit, and quietly reflected on their day. Reflection time is a good beginning of the year activity because it is quiet and easy to do. It trains the children to begin the lifelong process of thinking back on what has happened and using their reflections to help them plan for tomorrow. During reflection time, the teacher had time to look over the room and assess cleanup, time to think about what the children needed to do, and what they needed to bring to school the next day.

After they finished their reflections, the children put their books back in the trays where they kept their workbooks and gathered back on the carpet for the final sharing time. Sometimes in this sharing period they reviewed things from the day that would need to be carried over to the next day. For example, a play might need to be rescheduled or an assignment might take more work time. Sometimes unexpected things like programs interfered with work time and the children needed to know that they could still complete their work. Flexibility is essential. Louise asked them to think about what they needed to prepare for the next day. This was a final time for the group to reflect and for children to internalize the important messages from the day.

Reflections create metacognition. When children reflect they think back about their thinking. They consider how their planning helped them, the problems they encountered, and how they solved them. While their reflections often do not look particularly sophisticated, they are the first steps to thinking about thought and action.

The last message of the day was always positive. Louise might comment on how well they had worked, how smoothly cleanup had gone, or how much caring she had seen. Going home time needs ritual just as much as the beginning of the day does. Louise wanted each child to leave the class with good feelings. Talking about successes and their own plans for tomorrow created a friendly ritual of closure.

The time it takes to completely establish this daily routine will vary from a few weeks to perhaps a month depending on how quickly the teacher and the children develop their abilities to communicate with each other. The general outline is typically in place by the second or third day of school.

Working in New Ways

Throughout life the ability to manage time and balance conflicting demands is critical to happiness and productivity. Traditional classroom structures where children are told exactly what to do and when to do it do not teach children to plan responsibly or learn to manage their time. Many parents carefully structure their children's lives and take responsibility for being sure the children complete homework and do assigned tasks. However, children who are directed in this way may become passive and compliant or defiant or sometimes draggers of feet. The end results may not show up until high school, college, or entrance into the adult world.

The True Aim of Education

We agree with Kamii and Piaget that the true aim of education should be autonomy. We have a picture in our minds of a self-disciplined child who delights in learning, who understands how to take responsibility, and who knows how to work with others. These habits of mind take a lifetime to develop and many people leave school without having learned any of these vital life lessons.

In order to love learning, a child must have some voice in what is learned. Lessons must be relevant and meaningful. Learning must happen without coercion or penalty. The sheer excitement of acquiring new understanding needs to be stressed over the need to memorize information for tests. These conditions fly in the face of much conventional thinking about teaching and learning. They are based on the assumption that people are curious beings who learn because they want to know—not because someone bribes them in some way. These beliefs are supported by thinkers like Kohn (1993), Kamii (1985), Piaget (Wadsworth, 1978, 1984), Glasser (1998), and Zemelman et al. (1998).

Choices and Decisions Teach Responsibility

These same theorists support the premise that in order to teach someone to be responsible, it is necessary to give that person power to make choices and decisions, make mistakes, reflect, and grow from them. This is the essence of responsibility. Granted, the adults in charge need to establish limits and control choices to some extent. Adults also need to help children develop the ability to consider the pros and cons of different situations in order to make good decisions. A child who has always followed other people's directions may become a person who leaves home for college and flunks out because no one is there to tell him what to do.

Business leaders are also concerned with the problem of initiative. They report that many people come to work and wait to be told what to do next. Initiative is developed when children are given choice and responsibility. Children need to learn to work with other people in collaborative settings for the common good.

A powerful tool for Louise was the choices made available to her children. There were many things that children wanted to do in her room. The presence of the materials in the learning areas sent a message to the children that this teacher understood them and understood what kinds of things they wanted to do. Feeling understood led to more cooperation. Knowing that they had some control over their time meant that they took care of the givens more willingly. They did not want to waste their time and they knew that each person would be responsible for understanding the lessons Louise taught, so they listened attentively in large group sessions.

Living in a classroom that is becoming a community brings the great power of social relationships to learning. Group sharing of efforts gives students an audience beyond the teacher while honoring the differences in people.

Organizing Through Routines

The children must learn to organize their work, balance their time, and use it wisely. Their first impulse in the room is to play. Most people who visit the room and see the children building with blocks, pouring and measuring at the sand table, or creating things in the art center assume that the children are "just playing." At the beginning of the year, the children see assignments that must be done as obstacles to what they really want to do. As the year progresses, play and work gradually intertwine.

At the beginning of the year, however, the children must be taught about how to work thoughtfully, using varied materials in creative, imaginative ways. They need to make the transition from traditional classroom structures where they follow other people's directions all day to classroom structures that they help create. This transformation occurs gradually and naturally and the children are not really aware that they are making this transition.

Work That Looks Like Play

Louise worked hard at the beginning of the year to help the children know that they were actually doing work in the centers. The various areas in the classroom were full of raw materials for learning. While much of what happened looked like play, boundaries between work and play were blurred. One of the features that made the play serious, academic work was the requirement that the children write—to plan, record, and reflect on their activities. While the children had a natural tendency to explore and have fun with the materials, they had not yet been trained to think about or value what they were doing. Reporting on their activities later in the day made them more mindful of what they were doing and brought seriousness to their endeavors. This reporting happened mostly at the beginning of the year. There was less time for sharing things like investigations later in the year, as time became even scarcer due to the children sharing projects and publishing. Actually the work of investigations changed throughout the year. At the beginning of the year investigations taught children the tools they would need to develop projects. Later in the year when children worked on projects, they no longer needed to do as much work in their Investigations books. The children's time had to be balanced between givens and time for explorations and sharing with each other.

Home Learning Versus Formal Schooling

When people are infants, they work continuously to develop their skills. They work as hard as they can at rolling over, pulling up, and taking those first precious steps. The effort a baby puts in on a daily basis is astounding. All through the preschool period if they are given time and materials, children work towards increasing competence. They are continuously improving their skills. No one has to assign tasks for two-year-olds. They are constantly moving and learning. While parents and teachers try to keep children from doing things that are dangerous, they do not usually spend time telling them what to do.

When children begin formal schooling, life changes. No longer are they masters of their own time; no longer can they decide what to do and when to do it. And no longer do they work as hard as they can. Other people tell them what to do and other people watch to be sure that they at least attempt to do the tasks. Many of these tasks do not make sense to the children. Often in school, however, the children do just enough to please that omnipresent and omnipotent adult. Many children often become apprehensive and concerned about being able to do what is required and pleasing the teachers. Some children try to please and other children try to avoid too much notice. Most children's own agendas get buried in the day-to-day demands of school.

Developing Positive Dispositions Toward Learning

One of the things that Louise wanted to do was direct the children's natural enthusiasm and curiosity toward their schoolwork. She wanted to take the joy children have within them in playing and exploring the world and direct it through classroom structures where they could learn school curriculum from their explorations. She knew that working to please someone else is of limited long-term value (Kohn, 1993). She wanted children to develop a disposition to learn things related to academics (Bredekamp and Copple, 1997). School, done right, encompasses life and all its aspects. Louise sought to develop intrinsic motivation that would lead to lifelong learning. To accomplish this she focused children on owning and assessing their work in school.

The children needed to learn that recording in their Investigations books *was* their work. The year before, most of these children had completed many handout sheets and had considered those sheets to be their work. They liked getting check marks and carrying home sheaves of papers every day. Louise had to carefully explain that writing in their books was work just like doing worksheets. What she did not tell them was that they would be doing far more work in blank books than they had ever done on worksheets. In their blank books they had to do all the writing, draw all the lines, and construct any charts and graphs they might need. Open-ended assignments took more planning and thinking on the part of children and were sometimes frustrating to the children at the beginning of the year. They began to grow as they struggled with issues of creating, planning, and recording their work.

These assignments were designed to help children learn to read, write, and do math. Reading happened throughout each day as children were involved in their work. For example, they had to read in order to complete their givens. They had to read the game cards for the sharing time game; they had to read the charts that soon covered the walls of the room. They had to read the self-assessment guides that Louise put into their blank books. Reading and writing were inextricably linked. As the children read a variety of materials, they became better writers. As their writing improved, they became better readers.

Writing was required for many things in the room. The children wrote in their blank books in response to open-ended assignments. They wrote letters to each other in their dialogue journals. Sometimes when problems occurred they wrote to their parents to explain what had happened. They filled out forms to get jobs. Each child had folders for publishing. They made plans to do cooking, woodworking, or to use the fancy art materials such as feathers, googley eyes, or buttons in Creation Station. All day long children talked, read, and wrote, often without noticing that they were working.

The Foundation of the Community

The first weeks of school establish the foundation for any classroom community. Teachers who ignore the importance of this foundation may find themselves in classrooms where children resist learning and argue with each other and with the teacher. Many such classrooms are tight, narrow, and unstable because they do not focus on children.

The teacher's focus determines the nature of the foundation. Teachers who recognize the crucial significance of the beginning deliberately develop a sense of community. Teachers build their foundations on their beliefs about children and how they learn. Great teachers put children at the center of all they do. Creating community is hard work and takes thought. Teachers must know children, believe in them, be willing to try, make mistakes, reflect, and grow. The aim is to create communities that nurture all children and help them develop to their greatest potentials.

4

—

The First Weeks of School:
Learning About Quality

Fear is the lock, and laughter is the key to our souls.

—W. B. YEATS

When I arrived another morning a few days after school had begun, I found Ella in charge of the group time after sharing time. Louise had been called to a meeting. Good work habits take time to establish especially when children must learn to direct their own time. The teachers were beginning to train the children to complete several specific tasks each day. The children were learning to be responsible for managing their time during the day. They had a number of blank workbooks, each requiring different kinds of work. They had to use these books, such as their planners, investigations, or reading logs for recording their work. Some of the early tasks were designed to help the children develop skills they would need later in the year as they worked on projects. Soon the children would come to understand that time expectations could vary according to the needs of the child.

Ella reminded the children that many of them had not turned in their work the day before and that it was due today. She added, "It would be wise to plan so as to make sure your givens are completed on time." Louise and Ella expected that most of the children would not complete all those tasks in one day. They wanted them to realize that work not completed in a day could be finished another day without negative consequences. Later, both teachers would expect the work to be completed by an agreed upon time unless the student and teacher had conferenced and changed the date. The year had just begun and the children were not yet acclimated to the concept of time management.

Beginning Work Assignments

One of the first assignments involved having the children look closely at the animals in the classroom. At this point in the year, the classroom menagerie consisted of a snake, a couple of toads, frogs, a hamster, fish, and a tarantula (see Figure 4–1). The directions for the investigations assignment were still written on the board:

- Observe an animal in the class.
- Write a description of it.
- Describe its habitat.
- Record over a period of at least five minutes what it is doing.

This first assignment was designed to help the children begin the process of observing and recording. In addition, children were supposed to record and label shapes they found in the room. They were to write their numerals from one to one hundred. Based on the previous tour of the centers and the group discussion, the children were to write on the topic of "How to Use Centers." These tasks were also planned in order to get the children up and moving around the room. The aim was for children to begin using the rich materials in the class to accomplish directed work as well as for free explorations.

Figure 4–1. *The classroom menagerie.*

Some of these tasks were deliberately open-ended to permit each child to work to his or her highest level without fear of being wrong. Louise knows that young children are sometimes afraid to make mistakes. The open-ended tasks permit children to be challenged, not intimidated.

Louise's Reflections

Success on first tasks sets the tone for the year. I know children need challenge, but they also need to be able to succeed without continually tripping up. If the challenge requires too large a leap, they'll come crashing down. Children who are very afraid of making mistakes may just sit quietly and do nothing or invent things that get them into trouble.

The math assignment, writing numerals from one to one hundred, was not open-ended. Some assignments would not be. Even for this more traditional assignment, however, children were allowed to work together if necessary and the numbers were up on the wall on a hundreds chart for easy reference. Early tasks also helped the children develop good work habits. They needed to learn to follow directions, plan their time, work to their best effort, and take responsibility for their work.

Watching the children at work and reading their responses to these tasks told Louise a great deal about the children's strengths and abilities. Looking at the children's work provided her with some understanding of what each child could do. The writing assignments provided Louise with feedback as to how much the children had absorbed in their discussions on the use of centers. While none of these tasks were graded, written and oral feedback gave encouragement and suggestions for improvement.

Before letting them go to centers, Ella added, "If you are sure you have finished your givens, you may choose other work in centers." Working in centers meant choosing materials and equipment in a center and exploring possibilities. Work in centers involved choices like playing games on the computer, reading books, making something in art, building with blocks or Legos, writing a card to a friend, working with clay, or painting at the easel.

Louise's Reflections

Children want to learn and if we give them time, space, and some freedom to pursue their interests, they will surprise us with the results. I believe that my children learn as they explore and follow their interests in these varied activities during work time. I worked hard to make sure that each day included some time for the children to pursue these activities. Soon they would be focusing much of their time and interest on projects. Many of these activities help them develop and present their projects. Even as an adult, I don't like to focus every minute of my day. Sometimes, I need time to explore my world.

Working and Exploring All Over the Classroom

Just after group time, I went to sit at a table where Jason was writing about his experiences with the class spider. He explained that he needed spelling help and asked another child to tell him how to spell "tarantula." His method of getting help from a friend was acceptable.

In a few minutes, the spider investigator went off for more spelling help. He wrote "I like the tarantula the best. I would like to hold him. He is furry. He has 8 legs."

He returned and Louise came by and read the tarantula story. "Wonderful. Now what are you going to do with it? What else could you do with it?" This was an initial step in helping him consider ways to expand his work. The children learned from the beginning of the year that continuous improvement meant that their work efforts could be examined, expanded, and made better. When they learned about quality, they would begin to see how continuous improvement would help them grow. Helping the children think of ways to expand their work moved them toward more involvement in their own interests. This self-direction led to a deeper joy of learning.

Two boys played nearby in the sand. One girl objected, "You guys have been hogging it."

"There's always tomorrow," was the airy reply, "We can play as long as we want." The boys were correct. During the work times, there were no time limits on the use of centers. Louise believes that children need uninterrupted time using materials in order to be able to plan and carry out their plans. Most of the time this worked out well and the children did not abuse their privileges because they still had the responsibility of getting their givens done. Some givens could be done in areas like sand, water, or blocks but often givens required different types of materials in other centers. Most children moved on to other work anyway when they grew tired of what they were doing.

Chris came by looking for shapes in the room. He spelled out "square." David went over to the pegboard and shyly pointed out a circle on the bottom of a measuring cup.

Chris asked what I was doing. "I'm writing what happens so I can tell the story of the room," I replied.

He said, "Okay, why don't you write about the cooking center." He moved on.

Addressing Problems in the Classroom

"Listen," said Louise in a very serious voice that got everyone's attention. At the listen signal, children all over the room stopped what they were doing to attend to the teacher. "Someone was petting the hamster, and that was fine. But they left the top off the cage. What is the problem?" Louise presented the problem to the class so that they could consider the consequences and solutions.

The children discussed briefly what could happen if the hamster got loose. No blame was laid but everyone in the class was made to feel a responsibility for taking care of the animals. The children went back to work. This short incident focused the children on their collective responsibility for the room and all its inhabitants. This room could not operate well unless all the children cared for it. Helping them learn this lesson was best done with concrete examples and without blame or fear. Louise appealed to the thinking and feeling parts of each child.

Artistic Endeavors

Two painters had an audience of onlookers and people waiting for a turn. They were busy, but only two could use the easel at a time. Louise talked to me of the need for a place to dry the paintings. She planned to hang a line the next weekend. As the children used the room, Louise watched constantly to see what needed modifying in the environment.

Kimberly was painting a crazy world. "The sky's on the floor. The grass is blue. Crazy land," she mused as she used her fingernails to scratch lines in the wet paint. Yellow gold went on top and the sides were blue. Many varied materials allowed for rich creativity.

Kimberly finished and folded her bright picture of shapes and colors and put it under the easel. I doubted that folding improved her picture, but she had gotten it out of the way. Even for second graders, process may be as important as product.

Another child painted a picture of two hills with flowers, a tree, a blue cloud in the sky, a yellow sun in the corner, and a blue spot, which I assumed was a pond. The painting was joyful, bright, and relaxed. Its exuberance signaled the comfort and freedom the child felt.

Figure 4–2. *A child at the easel.*

The girls seemed to have exclusive use of the easel that morning (see Figure 4–2).

Chris came up to give advice. "Do you know what you need? See where you painted blue. It could have been black." The painters did not pay much attention to the advice.

Introducing the Concept of Quality

Helping children learn to direct themselves to work and play productively is neither automatic nor easy. A major tool in the shift in responsibility from teacher-directed to joint child-teacher-directed learning is found in the study of quality. Commitment to quality helps children move beyond just getting by or just pleasing the teacher. Quality is a key tool to help children develop good work habits. They use quality tools to evaluate their work and develop goals for improvement. A commitment to quality strengthens community and helps it function optimally. When children have choices and make decisions, they begin to feel in control of their lives and their learning. Their classroom must be a safe community where they are not made to feel afraid. Children need to feel comfortable and unafraid of grades, of voicing opinions, or of making mistakes. "No fear" is the necessary precondition to real engagement in the learning process.

Developing an understanding of quality takes time and constancy of purpose. In Louise's classroom the first steps toward quality started at the beginning of school when the teachers encouraged children to work to their best effort. The teachers helped the children understand that each child's effort would be different and acceptable. When Louise introduced the first work assignments, she also introduced key words and concepts that would be essential in working toward quality. Words like *responsibility, dependability, caring,* and *persistence* needed to be familiar to children before they could start working toward quality. The teachers frequently used these terms in context and the children gradually learned their meanings.

On this day after large group sharing, during teacher time, the actual word *quality* was introduced. Louise asked the question, "What is quality?" The children talked about what they thought the word meant. In early conversations they said things like, "Quality is doing something real good," "It's the best," or "Quality is perfect."

Louise showed the children two toy cars, one red and the other yellow. She asked them to talk about the quality of each car. The children looked both vehicles over. They thought that the details on the yellow plastic car were very good, but they found that it didn't roll very well. While the red car was made of metal and rolled fast, it was very plain. Then they decided that the plastic car would break easily while the red car would not. As they continued to examine the cars, they began to realize that each car had certain quality features but each was different. Then, when Louise asked if both were quality cars, the children said "Yes, but . . ." and started telling how each could be improved. Louise agreed and told them that if the toy makers heard the children's feedback, they would create higher quality cars.

Louise explained to them that quality in school, just like quality in the cars, is not based on being perfect. Working on quality meant that they would decide on indicators that would help them know what quality work looked like. Louise knew that their work included both academic and social learning. Just as the toy makers could improve their products, children could improve their work by using indicators to assess themselves, by responding to feedback, and by setting new goals.

Established Indicators

The children would come to understand that quality requires establishing indicators or standards for self-evaluation. Louise told the children that they would be developing quality indicators or standards to help them do quality work. It is not enough to tell a child, "Do your best" without helping the child come to an understanding of what his or her best would include.

A Continual Effort

In order to have improvement, students have to make effort. Effort is a critical part of success in life. Talking about quality means encouraging children to put their best efforts into everything they attempt. Without effort, improvement would happen very slowly, if at all. Improvement through effort brings change. When the children achieve their goals based on best effort, they are ready to set new goals for themselves. Achieving goals takes time. The time it takes for a child to achieve a goal varies according to the needs of that child. Each child needs to understand that accomplished goals should be maintained as new goals are added.

Improving

The children would learn that quality does not mean being perfect all the time but instead refers to improving (Bonstingl, 1992). The children loved the notion of improving as a line that goes on forever without end. Later, the metaphor became a ladder that goes up forever and ever. Climbing a ladder works best one rung at a time.

A Wow

The teacher explained to the children that when they had accomplished their goals, they would experience a "Wow!" "A 'Wow' happens when you have done the very best you can do or when you have learned something new for you." When a "Wow" is experienced, the next rung of the ladder is ready for climbing and new goals must be identified. Then the teacher and the children worked together to create their quality chart.

What is Quality?

- Established indicators
- A continual effort
- Improving
- A Wow!

Building a Quality Community

As the children were developing their community, working together with materials in the room, sharing personal experiences, solving problems, and talking about their work, they were also acquiring some of the vocabulary and understandings necessary for the next steps. The concepts of quality were deepened as the children and their teachers developed a shared vision, set class goals, created systems for organizing the room, developed an understanding of class government, and established quality indicators.

Vision

After the initial discussions about what quality meant, the class began the work of developing their shared vision. Louise asked the children, "Why are you coming to school this year?" Their first answers were broad and somewhat vague: "I want to learn." "I want to make good grades." "I want to do good for my mom and dad." "I want to be smart." "I want to pass." "My mama and daddy have to go to work." As they answered, the teacher recorded their responses on the board. Then she led them into discussing the things that they felt were really important about school. She listed their thoughts on the board. Using these thoughts, Louise and the children worked to develop their shared vision for the year.

At this time the word *consensus* was introduced. They learned that consensus meant that people worked together until everyone was satisfied. Consensus was not winning by voting (majority rules) or having a few children give in. Compromise that happens when someone agrees because of intimidation or peer pressure is not part of consensus. Three or four drafts were generated before the children voted on their vision statement. Usually the first vote was not unanimous. However, for an issue as important as the class vision, all the children needed to agree that they could live with the final version. Louise asked the children who voted differently from the majority, "What would you need to add or change to make this one acceptable to you?" After more discussion and changes to the statement, they voted again. At last they had their vision of what they wanted from school this year. The children had learned that consensus takes time.

Our Class Vision
Our vision for this year is to learn, have fun, and grow.

Goals

Louise knew that the children needed to have more specific goals that gave more guidance to the general vision they had developed. After developing their vision, the children were asked individually to write about some of their goals for the year. Upon completing their writing, the class met as a group to share what they had written individually. They discovered that many of their goals were similar. Louise explained that they would need to develop class goals to help them work toward their vision. The children worked together to develop long-term class goals based on some of their individual goals. Their individual goals were not discarded but were filed in their working portfolios for later review. More specific goals for individual children would emerge later in relation to their academic and social development.

Classroom Goals

Friendly	Courteous	Listen	Fair	Independent
Respectful	Helpful	Patient	Question	Responsible
Honest	Plan	Priority	Learn	Dependable
Self-control	Effort	Quality	Positive	Persistent

This whole procedure did take time but it taught so much. Children learned what democracy meant by participating in establishing a group vision and goals. They also learned to come to consensus as they respected the different opinions of others. This was real-life social studies. They learned to voice and defend their opinions in a respectful manner. Many adults find this difficult. The process of developing a vision and goals honored differences and these differences were incorporated into the final product. Children were learning what it takes to respect other people's opinions and to care for other people even if their beliefs are different. Honoring children's differing convictions empowered them.

This process helped to foster the growth of self-discipline and empowered the students. Students began learning that self-control lay within themselves. Teachers can guide but ultimately each student must choose how to behave, how to work, and how to learn.

Metacognition was also developing as this process evolved. Children were being asked to think about their thinking and how they worked best. The development of metacognitive skills occurs slowly throughout the elementary years. Children's future success in school is often created by their abilities to analyze their learning strategies, use their preferred learning styles, and to self-evaluate as they work to improve. The roots of these processes lie in the kinds of discussions Louise had with her children at the beginning of the year and throughout the year. These discussions were designed to create empowerment and foster the desire to learn and improve.

Organization Makes the Difference: Systems Theory

The concept of total quality is built on the notion that systems or plans for getting things done must be established for any work to be done efficiently. When there are problems in the classroom or workplace, students trained in quality do not point fingers of blame, but instead examine the systems that are in place. The question is not "Who is to blame?" but "Why is the system not working?" Systems that work best are those created by the workers or students. When problems arise in the workplace or classroom, the people best suited to solve the problems are the people involved. As the children learned about quality, they learned to look at modifying systems to solve problems and bring improvement. In Louise's classroom, systems changed in response to problems or because the teacher and children were looking for ways to continuously improve.

By the end of the first weeks of school, the children and their teachers had talked about many systems: systems for sharing, for getting materials, for using materials, for moving in the class and in the building, for cleanup, and for interaction. Some systems dealt with one step like the use of the word *listen* to get people's attention. The children were taught that when anyone said "listen" they were to stop, look to the person talking, think about what the person was saying, and understand what the speaker had said. Others, like cleanup, would have many steps. When the children started using centers, the need for a system for cleanup arose. In large group, the children developed a flowchart for cleanup (see Figure 4–3).

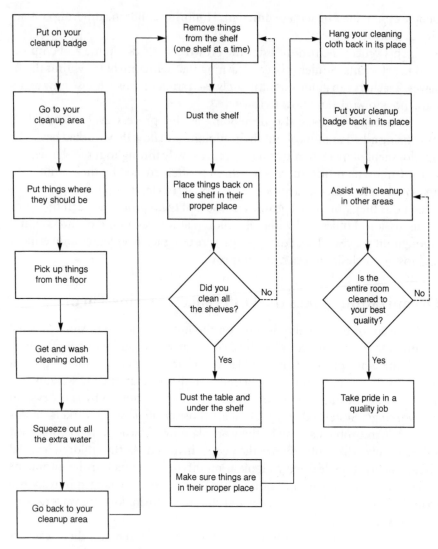

Figure 4-3. *The cleanup flowchart.*

Governing Themselves

When problems arose, Louise's goal was to help children learn to solve their problems on their own. Most small problems were resolved quickly and individually. The key to problem solving is clarification of the issues and finding solutions without blaming anyone. Children often came to Louise wanting arbitration. They wanted her to tell them who was right and what to do. She turned the responsibility back over to them by asking, "What is the problem? What caused it? How do *you* plan on solving it?"

Cleanup often produced the biggest problems at the beginning of the year. Few children had been trained to take the kind of responsibility Louise expected. If the children were to use the room, they had to learn to care for it. Sand and water on the floor, art material scattered over the art center, blocks not classified correctly, and books lying around were common problems at the beginning of every year.

After using learning areas for several days, cleanup concerns became evident. Several children came running up to Louise to report that the trash in the bathroom trash can was wet and that the floor was also wet. Louise gathered the children together, "I hear you saying that we are having cleanup problems. I have a chart that my students have used in the past. Perhaps what we need is to review this problem solving chart." Ella went to the closet and got the chart and then Louise shared the chart with the class (see example in Figure 4–4).

The first step on the chart was to identify the problem. The children described the problem. The next step was talking about what caused the problem. The children soon realized that some people had not wrung out their cleaning cloths after using them and water had dripped on the floor and in the trash basket. The next step was to brainstorm strategies for preventing the problem from reoccurring. One of their plans was to be careful to wring out their cleaning cloths and the other was to appoint an inspector to check to be sure that none of the cloths were dripping. They decided to try both strategies. This problem was easily solved; the dripping cloths ceased to be a problem. The problem solving chart was then used throughout the year to help solve individual or group problems. It was placed in the sharing area for easy reference, especially during large group meetings.

Council Meetings

This informal meeting set the stage for the development of a key element in the classroom government—the council meeting. The formal council meetings evolved from early decision making discussions like the one we just described. First meetings of the council were often informal and called by the teacher as the need arose. Class meetings were held to celebrate each other's successes as well as to solve problems. For instance, when Frank, a child who had previously experienced little school success, drew a picture of a dog and trees early in the year, Louise called the group together to appreciate and celebrate

Problem Solving

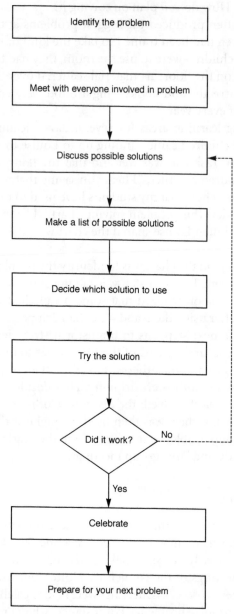

Figure 4–4. *A problem solving chart.*

his efforts and his work. Not only did he gain confidence; the other children experienced the satisfaction of helping a classmate succeed.

After several meetings of this kind, the teacher suggested that they needed a way to communicate as a group. She talked about how the local community was governed. The children went on a field trip to the courthouse to meet the mayor and other government officials. The group would later use many of the words they learned on the field trip to help create their own government systems.

The council was the main governing body for the fledgling government. The council established a weekly meeting time. The children or teachers could also call emergency meetings when needed. All members of the class served on the council. Each child and each teacher had one vote. During council meetings, the children sat in a circle with the secretary and assistant in the middle.

Applying for Jobs   After Louise conducted several meetings the children applied for various positions, and based on their applications, were appointed to positions. Terms were variable and were decided more by circumstances such as illness, school vacations, or maybe a big snow than by a fixed-time schedule. Flexibility was the key. Positions included a mayor to take charge at the meeting and an assistant mayor who recorded issues on the board and was in charge when the mayor was absent. A secretary and an assistant were responsible for taking minutes at each meeting. Taking minutes was a hard job and could make people's fingers hurt. Sometimes an assistant had to take over mid-meeting.

Uses of Meetings   After the council was established, children began to see the council meetings as a place to help and care for others while resolving problems that arose in the room. Council meetings were also held to plan parties, field trips, their birthday celebrations, and activities for student teachers. The group worked together on a flowchart (see Figure 4–5, p. 92) to reflect the basic agenda for their meeting.

Class Government

The class government was broader than just the council. Near the beginning of the year, Ella created a class government chart based upon needs that had been identified by the class. Each child needed a job for the government to run smoothly. Every person was responsible for some of the activities of the room. Each child's name was on a small piece of paper backed with Velcro so

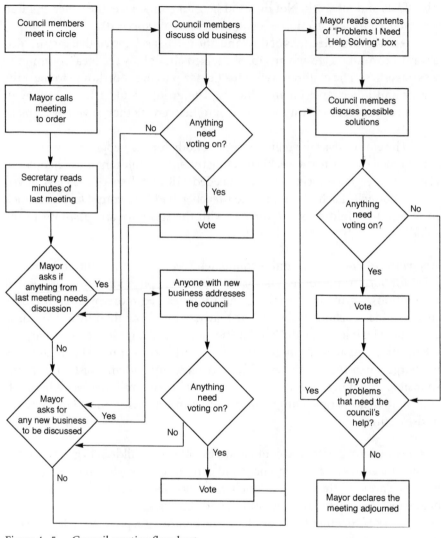

Figure 4–5. *Council meeting flowchart.*

that the names could be changed easily. The class government consisted of the following jobs:

Mayor/Assistant Mayor
In charge of Council

Host/Hostess
Greet visitors
Conduct tours
Camera

Postmaster/Assistant
Mailing
Sell stamps
Stamping

Secretary/Assistant
Record minutes
Write "Thank You"
  notes
Bulletin boards

Reporter/Assistant
Take notes for articles
Newspaper

Treasurer/Assistant
Collect money
Record bank
  transactions
Report to Council

Animal Control Officer/Assistant
Closet
Feed animals
Record feedings
Clean cages
Keep clean water

Health Inspector/ Assistant
Trays
Mailboxes
Keep records and
  reports

Building Inspector/ Assistant
Cleanup
Keep records of
  assessment

Employment Commissioner/ Assistant
Set change deadlines
Review applications
Fill positions

Planning Board
Plan parties
Agendas
Run store
In charge of parties

The children found real reasons for writing when they filled out application forms for the positions they wanted. Each position required children to use various types of writing for record keeping. They began to see that people write for many purposes. The government allowed the children to take on real responsibilities as well as solve real problems as they happened. Through these processes, such as the secretary's report in Figure 4–6, the children felt empowered—in control of themselves and of the room.

Establishing Quality Indicators

Self-evaluation is key to the process of continuous improvement. The children learned that through the process of self-evaluation they would set new goals. The children developed these goals based upon their self-assessment and the indicators that they had helped to establish.

This process is very different than trying to get all the answers correct. The aim of most assignments was to give children many opportunities to read and write and think about what they did. In everything they did, they were encouraged to celebrate success but also challenged to identify ways to improve their work as they continued to make progress. Taking responsibility meant learning to assess their own work rather than waiting for the teacher to put a smiley face or a grade on what they had done.

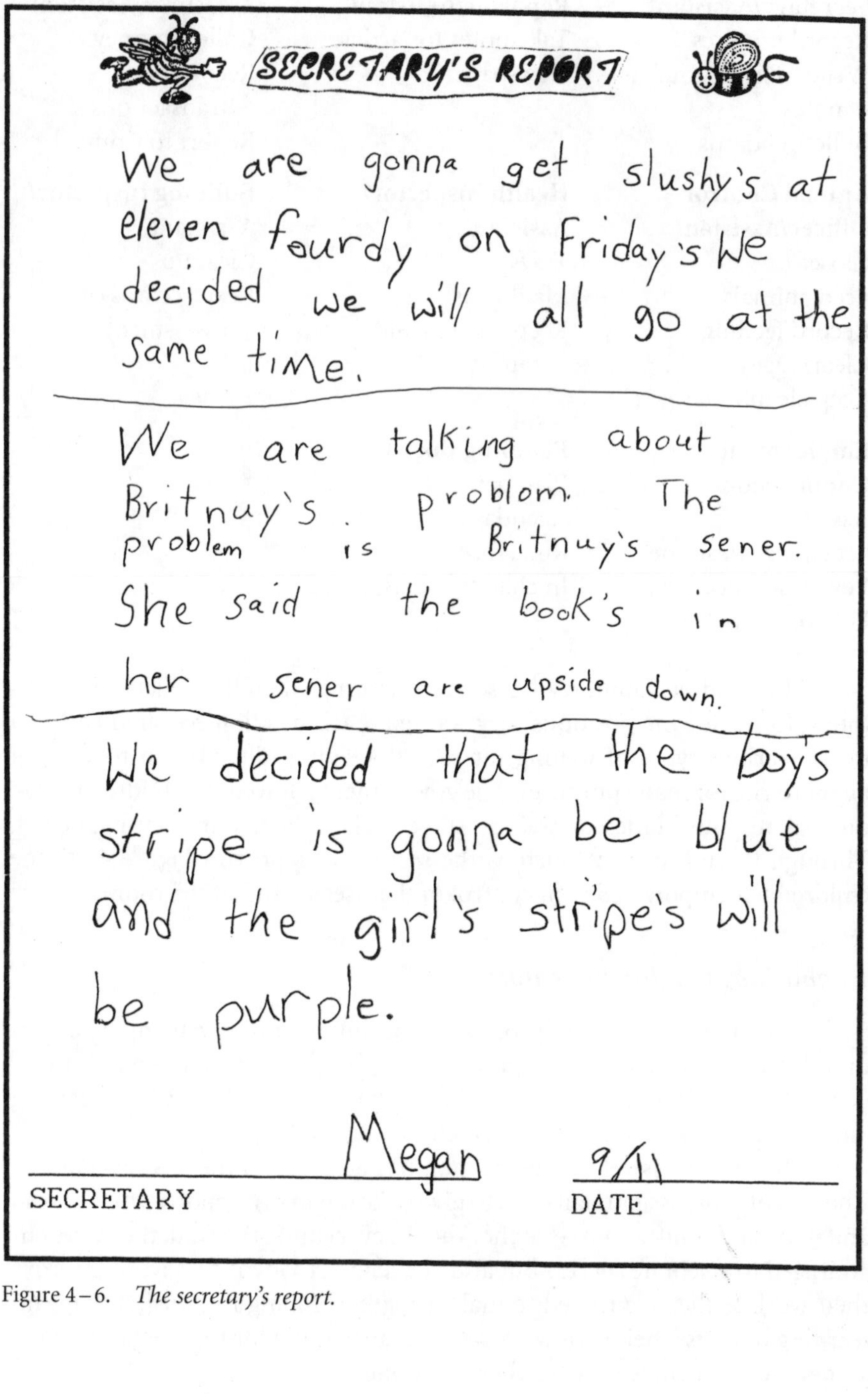

SECRETARY'S REPORT

We are gonna get slushy's at eleven fourdy on Friday's We decided we will all go at the same time.

We are talking about Britnuy's problom. The problem is Britnuy's sener. She said the book's in her sener are upside down.

We decided that the boy's stripe is gonna be blue and the girl's stripe's will be purple.

Megan

SECRETARY

9/11

DATE

Figure 4–6. *The secretary's report.*

Louise's Reflections

The children would soon realize that factors such as amount of time they had available, being ill, or other personal problems would have an impact on their ability to exert high quality effort all the time. As a teacher, I tried to be aware that working for continuous improvement had to be seen as a whole over a period of time. Continuous progress doesn't necessarily mean smooth, constant effort. When climbing a tall ladder, a person often needs to take a break before taking the next step. Sometimes it helps to move back a step in order to refocus. Once in a while we all have "down days" even on the road to continuous improvement. Through observing and interacting with my children, I was better able to know when one of them had a "down day" or when one needed encouragement to make more effort.

After becoming acquainted with the term *quality,* designing their vision and goals, and establishing the class government the next step was to establish quality indicators to help the children self-evaluate and set their own goals.

Louise's Reflections

The children and I worked together to develop indicators in various areas as they were needed. There were three main charts that seemed to always come first. They were very important in helping the children to function in their community. We placed the charts on the wall near the sharing area in the classroom. They would be referred to many times throughout the year. They were the quality indicator charts for listening, speaking, and encouragement.

A GOOD LISTENER
Quality Indicators

- Sits quietly
- Looks at the speaker
- Thinks about what the speaker is saying
- Is patient
- Doesn't change the subject
- Doesn't interrupt
- Can reflect back on what was said

A GOOD SPEAKER
Quality Indicators

- Speaks loud enough
- Looks at listeners
- Uses expression
- Uses motions to match expressions
- Doesn't change subject
- Makes sure listeners understand
- Asks questions
- Discusses when needed

ENCOURAGING OTHERS
Quality Indicators

Things we say . . .

- I like the way you used expression . . .
- I like the way you illustrated . . .
- I like the book you picked . . .
- I like that suggestion . . .
- That's a good idea . . .
- I'd like to hear what you think about . . .

Things we do . . .

- Smile
- Pat on the back
- Nod
- Look at the person
- Show expression
- Use a friendly tone of voice
- Clap
- Write a note

When the children began sharing their written work, the need for quality indicators also became apparent to the teacher. She could see that the children needed guidance in their writing. They developed these quality indicators as a group when they discussed samples of work from previous years. (A beginning teacher might need to go to another teacher and borrow old work samples.) Louise read a sample of work from a child who was in her class last year. The child's name had been removed. Louise showed the children the illustrated story and asked them "Did you enjoy the story?"

The children were positive. They quickly answered, "It was good." Louise agreed. She knew that children at this stage had had little experience in actually responding to anyone's work. They were not sure what to say about someone else's story.

"I liked the story, too. Would there be any suggestions that you could make to help improve the paper?" Louise wanted the children to begin to think critically about what makes quality written work. She knew that the children would not immediately identify all the things that would bring improvement. They began by pointing out simple things like no period at the end of the sentence and problems with spacing of letters and words. They noticed the mechanical parts of the writing such as periods, spacing, margins, and work dated rather than the content. The things they noticed were probably things that had been marked on their own papers last year.

Louise was pleased with their initial efforts. "Wow, you have good suggestions. I think your suggestions could make good indicators for quality in written work." They worked together to draft a list of indicators for written work. Louise knew that the list would grow, as the children grew in their abilities. None of the beginning indicators would necessarily be dropped.

Quality Indicators for Written Work

- Spacing of letters and words
- Size of letters and words
- Formation of letters
- Correct letters capitalized
- Punctuation marks used in correct places
- Margins
- Work dated
- Best spelling effort
- Neat
- Work completed on time

Quality Indicators for Work Behaviors

- Plans with details
- Completes plans
- Starts right to work

- Self-directed
- Shares tools and work space
- Completes work on time
- Respects others
- Returns materials to their proper places

As the children created quality indicators for their work the process focused them on what they needed to do in their work. Since they understood that quality meant continuous progress, they knew that indicators were standards by which they could assess their work and establish their goals. The students learned to use the quality indicators when the teacher conferenced with them individually and in group sharing times.

After the children developed the charts for quality work, they developed the indicators for self-directed learning. These indicators are the keys to helping children become responsible, caring citizens of their community. Later in the year, the children would conference with the teacher every two weeks, self-assess based on the indicators, and establish new goals. Each child would respond to these prompts: "I feel good about . . ."; "I learned . . ."; "My goals for next week are . . ." Each child assessed himself or herself based on these indicators and planned for improvement.

Quality Indicators for Self-Directed Learners

- Makes plans
- Sets goals
- Completes priorities
- Sticks to task
- Works for accuracy
- Assumes responsibility for actions
- Completes work on time
- Works cooperatively with others
- Is sensitive to feedback
- Monitors and assesses progress
- Shows respect
- Takes responsibility
- Shows caring
- Pushes to learn more
- Makes products that achieve their purpose
- Tries new ways of doing things

These were things that Louise knew that all the children could do with effort. Other indicators for such areas as reading, projects, and math would be developed later.

Shared Assessments

Assessment was jointly shared by the child and teacher as they reviewed the work during an individual conference. Other times during a work sharing session, the whole class provided feedback to the student who was sharing. Much of this feedback was based on indicators that the class had previously established. The children understood feedback as a way of helping others by providing possible suggestions for improvement. The class knew that the decision as to whether or how to use this feedback was the responsibility of the student who had shared. Thus, the public conversations about work in progress were nonthreatening. Mistakes or problems meant that improvement could be made rather than that a child had failed or was stupid. This sharing helped the children respect work done at different levels. Quality meant "It is okay for you to work at your own level, you will be improving and growing as you learn. Learning is continuous just like climbing the ladder."

Louise's Reflections

I discussed with the children their differences in heights. Then I told them the story of a boy I'd known when I was in high school. He was much shorter than me all through our years in school. Several years after graduation, when I met him, he towered ten inches above me. I explained to the children that learning also occurs like this. We are in different stages of development in reading, writing, and math. As time passes, we change. Many people learn to do things well that they couldn't do before. This change is up to us. Our efforts make changes possible.

A Sharing Session

At the beginning all the children needed to be called on to share. This took a long time and sessions in which everyone had a turn were only held a few times at the beginning of the year. After these first few sessions, the teacher might randomly select only five or six students a day to share. Records of which children had had a turn were essential. All children needed to have a chance to share some work before starting the process again. During large group sharing, children who had forgotten about quality in their written work found themselves at sharing time with incomplete work. When called upon, they tried to explain why the work wasn't finished. When the group looked to the quality indicators, then the children realized that their work did not reflect their best efforts. When caring children offered suggestions for ways to improve, the reality of the group's expectations and the importance of the quality indicators hit home. Looking at work as a group allowed children to learn how to assess their work and effort in a positive way. They learned how to give and receive constructive feedback to help people learn and grow. These sharing sessions happened frequently at the beginning of the year and less frequently when the children understood how to work toward quality.

By going over the work in a public setting, shared expectations were being developed. One afternoon in September, Louise began the sharing session with Elizabeth. Elizabeth read what she had written and showed her work to the group. The children first pointed out things that they liked and then made suggestions for improvement. Several children questioned her use of margins and Alice said that she had not included enough details. Louise pointed out Elizabeth's quality printing. Helping the children look for positive qualities in their work was the teacher's responsibility.

Louise guided the group process. She wanted the children to be able to make and take constructive suggestions given in a caring way. The next child, Timothy, was very hesitant about standing up in front of the group to share. He whispered that he did not get to finish the last line. His previous teacher had reported that he said little the entire year. He needed extra support here at the beginning of a new school year.

Louise reassured him. "It sounded really interesting. You had the date, neat printing, and good margins." She began with the quality indicators that she felt each child could achieve at the beginning—margins, date, and careful printing. Later, she moved toward increasing awareness of content and structure.

She found a period at the end of his last sentence and suggested that he *did* finish. Based on Louise's reactions, the group decided that he had done a good job. The children learned how to find the good in other people's work by watching and listening to their teacher.

All of the children's work was different. The children searched Louise's face and words for clues as to how to react to each other's work. They were still trying to absorb the reasons behind the quality indicators. They were trying to apply simple quality standards to a complex process.

The teacher and the children looked at Robert's work. He had written five lines. "Did you finish?" asked Louise.

Chris remarked that Robert had his date, his margins, and interesting things to say.

Tina added, "I think he tried to do his best."

Kimberly agreed, "He worked really hard and he did his best."

Another child disagreed because the lines weren't straight enough. Jax concurred, and thought Robert should do a little bit more and add more details.

Self-evaluation was a vital part of the process. Louise asked Robert, "Do you think you did your best?"

"Yes," he replied.

"I agree," said Louise. "Robert, you might want to consider Jax's suggestion of adding details as one of your new goals to work toward in your writing."

Louise addressed the whole group. "As you listen, try to think of things *you* can improve in your own work or ways that it might help you expand your work. Look at the indicators."

Louise always sat next to the child who stood to present the work. Often her arm was around the smaller shoulder for support. She forestalled the "That isn't good enough" process by quickly pointing out where the child had made progress and what had been done right. Her voice was warm, positive, and encouraging.

"I forgot my book. I didn't have time." For those who presented these excuses, Louise's voice held a note of sternness and challenge.

Excuses were problems that could have been solved. "You had a problem. What could you have done? What will you do next time?" she questioned. The group often suggested strategies that could help "next time."

The whole class was the audience for the presentation of student work. The audience had to be respectful. No one was allowed to snicker or point blaming fingers. Louise taught, "We help each other in this class." Dignity and respect were at the core of this process and Louise was very careful to preserve fragile, developing feelings of confidence. Children might finish their presentations feeling they needed to do more next time, but no one left feeling belittled or less of a person.

Each child's work was different. Many had only a few laboriously printed lines while others filled pages with details and descriptions. The key in this sharing was to be flexible and not to expect the same end product from everyone, but to continue expecting each student to work toward quality. Louise constantly emphasized the development of the process and the skills that would eventually yield a quality product.

Sharing time also allowed children to see the infinite possibilities inherent in the open-ended assignments as well as learn to be responsible. As each child shared, the children heard and saw other ways to do their work. Imagination and risk taking were valued and celebrated. Variations in products were validated.

Learning Self-Control

The process by which children learned to direct and control themselves took time and effort. It started at the beginning of the school year and was reinforced daily and weekly as new responsibilities were added and taught. Accountability through quality (by both the children and Louise) helped the children experience greater success.

There are many developmental stages and many barriers to developing self-direction in children. The children have to understand what is required in their work. This understanding takes TIME, especially when children are used to being told what to do and when to do it. Even the expectation that they will make wise choices about time use and complete their givens can be a shock to children. Self-control takes many people a lifetime to develop, so it should not surprise anyone that it is not innate in children.

Louise's Reflections

Many people think that if you tell a child something once, he should quickly change. We look for the magic words that will make problems disappear immediately. Children who obey and are compliant are seen as the good kids. The children who don't do what is wanted often get labeled as problem children or even "bad." I have never met a "bad" child. As we work with children, helping them to learn, grow, and develop, we need to be patient and understanding. We just need to remind ourselves that change takes time for children and grown-ups.

Choice One and Choice Two

One recurrent problem in most classrooms is children's unwillingness or inability to focus and complete their work. Under all types of classroom structures, teachers struggle with ways to MAKE children do their work. In *Choice Theory in the Classroom*, Glasser and Dotson (1998) remind us that no one can make another person do anything. Teachers can only persuade or encourage students by helping them see how what they are asked to do will meet their basic needs. In addition, we understand that even when children want to do their work, they may lack the skills of self-management necessary to complete everything on time. They may need help learning to manage their time effectively. This does not occur quickly. Instant results are not likely to happen. There are no magic phrases or quick fixes for the life lessons children need to learn.

Several years ago, Louise had a little boy named Ted in her class who challenged all the systems in her room. He never accepted responsibility for his actions; he always blamed the teacher or another child for causing him to have problems, particularly in terms of completing his work. After trying many strategies, including council meetings, in frustration Louise placed him in an assigned seat to complete his givens. He sat in the seat but he did not work. Force rarely produces quality work, and in this case, this child seemed to enjoy the power struggle.

During this time, the principal visited the room and asked Ted why he was in an assigned seat. Ted answered angrily, "Because Mrs. Burrell put me here." She overheard his remark. She thought to herself, "No, I didn't." At that point she realized that his real problem was that he was blaming everyone but himself. She *knew* that he had put himself there by his own actions based on his choices and decisions. However, he did not understand that his actions had put him in this position. In his mind, all the other people in the room had caused his problems. His behavior would not change until he accepted ownership of his behavior.

Louise wanted a way to help Ted learn to stop blaming others and to take responsibility for his actions. That night she went home and created a new flowchart to emphasize to Ted and to the other children the nature of the choices they were making (see Figure 4–7, p. 104). She wanted the children to understand that they made their own choices and decisions about completing their work. She wanted the children to understand that they controlled themselves. Basically, if children completed their work to quality they could choose when and where to do their subsequent work. In Choice One the child was in charge of completing all work and managing time.

If at conference the child and teacher realized that work was left undone, or not his best effort, then that child had chosen Choice Two. Choice Two was not a punishment. It was an acknowledgement that the child needed help and that the teacher cared enough to help him focus. Under Choice Two, the teacher met with the child and supplied the work, materials, and checked for quality at the end of each completed assignment. Choice Two meant the teacher helped the child get his givens done. After one assignment was completed, the child would be allowed to move around or work in the areas for a specified amount of time. The child was in charge of reporting back to the teacher to complete his work.

Louise's Reflections

I designed the chart not as a hard and fast rule or a "get-you" mechanism. Choice Two was not a punishment. I didn't want to use it in an inflexible way. It always depended on the needs of individual children. To me, children are more important than any system or chart. Choice Two was meant as a way for me to help the children learn to manage themselves and their time. It was also meant as a way for children to take responsibility for what they had or hadn't done. It was very powerful because the children wanted to be in charge of their time.

In the large group, Louise helped the children understand that emergencies happen and that emergencies or interruptions would not move a child from Choice One to Choice Two. Cases of emergency—being sick, going to

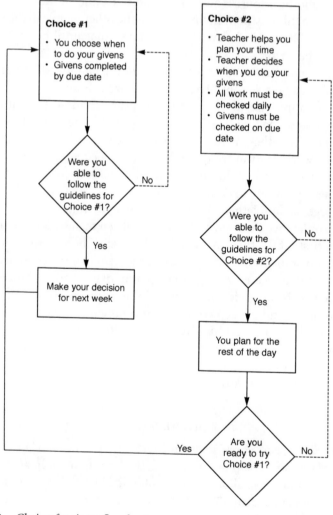

Figure 4–7. *Choices for givens flowchart.*

the dentist—might interrupt the completion of their work. Also, if Louise felt that a child had put good effort into her work but had not quite completed it or had forgotten to complete something, she might ask the child to identify strategies she might use to bring her work to quality by the next conference. The child would be left on Choice One. Planning these working strategies prevented many children from ever going to Choice Two at all. The key to successful implementation of this system was the teacher's reflective, thoughtful decision making and flexibility.

The chart was not a sure cure and was only one way that responsibility was developed. Children did not learn to be responsible immediately. Some children went back and forth between the two choices. However, each time they went back and forth, their time on Choice One got longer. Eventually, most of them worked exclusively on Choice One and managed their own time. As the children moved back and forth between the choices, the teacher helped them with the specific skills they needed.

Once the chart was introduced, Ted had to face himself and begin to accept his responsibilities. This took work and time.

Ted came to his conference with Louise complaining that he didn't have his work and that it was Joey's fault. He said Joey had kept him from completing his work.

Louise's first question was, "How did he keep you from doing your work?"

Ted replied angrily, "He was talking to me."

"What did you do about it?"

Ted gave her a sullen look.

"Did you ask him to stop?"

"No, I forgot," he admitted.

"Could you have moved to a different location to work?"

"But, but I was there first!" Ted spluttered.

"Did you ask for help?"

Ted looked frustrated. "Joey was bothering me," he complained again.

"Did he keep you from moving? What did you do about the problem?"

Eventually, this kind of dialogue also helped focus Ted on his own behavior. He stopped placing blame on others for his lack of responsibility. The new system took his wiggle room away. He wasn't cured overnight, but he made a lot of progress.

Reflections on Quality

Concepts of quality are useful for all ages. When first introduced to quality, adults will develop definitions and understandings of quality similar to those the children produced. They often focus on doing "perfect work." However, the concept of continuous improvement is much more useful than the idea of perfection. When people accept the challenge to continuously improve themselves, then they begin to grow.

Quality takes away competition in academic work. As children compete for doing the best work, making the highest grade, they lose their focus on learning. When quality guides the process, children work to improve in relation to themselves based on their own goals rather than in competition with others.

Any group is wise to take time to develop joint vision and goal statements. These will have power only when the participants take the process seriously and develop them together. Participants must have faith that their input will make a difference in the operation of the group. Consensus and community are not easy tenets to live by.

The processes we have described in this chapter will lead to self-discipline, self-management, accountability, and metacognition. These are skills that will result in full, productive lives for the people who learn them and a better world for all of us. Teaching these life skills needs to be a part of education at all levels. If all our citizens worked toward these things, our society would not be plagued with problems of violence, neglect, and indifference.

At any level, identification of the givens and quality indicators will make people focus on what they are doing. Understanding the reasons behind the givens will make people more willing to cooperate and do what is necessary.

If we could make one change in the world, it would be to help people learn to solve problems cooperatively. People who solve conflicts with words not weapons would create a world we would like to live in and a world where we could all feel safe. Problem solving is a vital life skill that is best learned in the context of real-life problems. A problem solving approach must be practiced daily with reflection, willingness to change, and care for others.

Council meetings or classroom meetings are powerful vehicles for working toward all these goals and for teaching democracy. The meetings will not work if they are contrived and artificial. The children involved need to know they have control, that their voices are heard, and that their suggestions will make a difference. They need to know that each child will be respected, treated fairly, and valued by the teacher. Trust in the teacher as well as the other children is the foundation on which community is developed.

Any elementary classroom built around the things children are interested in will be a powerful motivational tool (see Figure 4–8). Choice One and Choice Two allowed the power of the room help children make good choices.

Systems theory explains that we must look to the systems in place to improve the work we do. Every classroom has systems, but in many classrooms

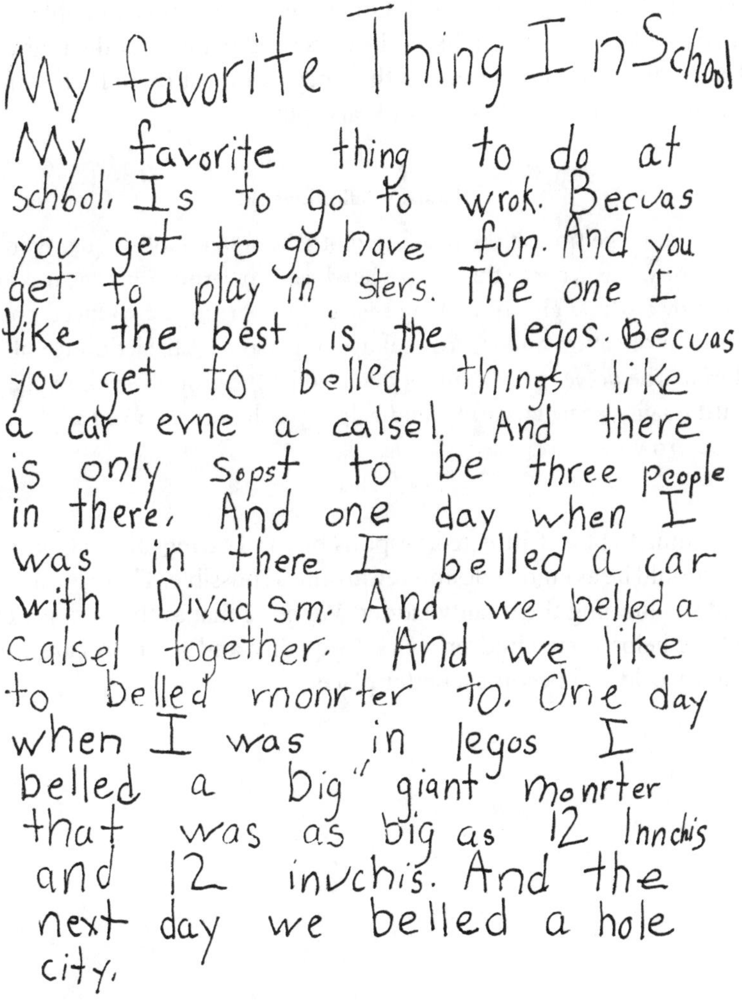

My favorite Thing In School

My favorite thing to do at
school. Is to go to wrok. Becuas
you get to go have fun. And you
get to play in sters. The one I
like the best is the legos. Becuas
you get to belled things like
a car evne a calsel. And there
is only sopst to be three people
in there. And one day when I
was in there I belled a car
with Divad sm. And we belled a
calsel together. And we like
to belled monrter to. One day
when I was in legos I
belled a big" giant monrter
that was as big as 12 Inndchis
and 12 invchis. And the
next day we belled a hole
city.

Figure 4–8. *My Favorite Thing in School shows how interested students stay more involved.*

the systems have evolved without thought and without awareness of their existence. Problems occur and people blame other people when they should be looking to the unidentified systems that control the work they do.

Quality is elusive. No one ever achieves total quality because the quest for it is continuous. Quality spirals with children through the grades. Each year, old indicators need to be reviewed and new indicators must be added as work becomes more sophisticated. This is the essence of continuous progress. Louise and I have used quality indicators with college students as well as elementary children. They have served us well. Quality indicators focus people on what good work looks like. The quality indicators need to be set at the highest possible level. All children need to feel that they can meet these high standards. Furthermore, each child's best effort is acceptable.

Louise's Reflections

While it did take time at the beginning of school to establish quality in the community, the synergy that was created was powerful. Synergy, the force created by a whole group working together in harmony, produced greater intrinsic motivation and strong feelings of personal satisfaction for all the children. The power of community created by the group working together toward quality, sharing, caring, and helping each other allowed all the children to grow.

Learning to be self-directed, responsible, and caring takes a lifetime. The journey should be as enjoyable and rewarding as possible. There is fun and excitement in climbing the quality ladder. We hope that as the next generation of teachers helps their children work to quality and learn to care for each other, our world will become a better place.

5
▬

Roadblocks, Yes Buts,
and Challenges for the Future

Nothing will ever be attempted if all possible objections must first be overcome.

—SAMUEL JOHNSON

During all the years that Louise was teaching, people often told her why she couldn't do what she was doing and why other people couldn't possibly teach the way she taught. First people said she was too young and inexperienced. Then they pointed out that she had no children of her own and that was why she had the time to try all these new things. Later, after she had a child, people began to say "But you have accumulated so much stuff. I can't afford to get all those books and materials." Then they would say, "Of course it is easy for you, because you have so much experience!" In the last few years, many people were convinced that what Louise advocates is impossible because of the increased emphasis on state testing.

All the while when people told Louise that she couldn't, she continued to work and work and do what she thought was right for children. She wasn't loud, and she didn't argue, but she persevered and did it her way. Over the years her way worked. She made many mistakes, solved many problems, and moved on. She taught her children that "mistakes are stepping stones to learning" and she lived this philosophy daily. Each problem became an opportunity to improve. As a result, after more than thirty years of teaching, Louise was still having a good time when she retired. The joy of learning has stayed with her.

Louise's Reflections

I have left the classroom but I am not really retired—now I work with student teachers and new teachers. I have discovered a whole new world, new problems, and new challenges. I am exploring a new frontier and I am excited. Helping student teachers work with their cooperating teachers and learn the basics of management and organization stretches me and makes me look for ways to adapt the strategies I've used for so many years. I continue to learn and explore the processes of teaching.

Louise's methods are congruent with the recommendations of national organizations such as the National Council of Teachers of Mathematics, National Council for Teachers of English, and the organizations for science and social studies. Zemelman et al. (*Best Practice,* 1998) cite a list of principles common to most of these major organizations. These groups urge teachers to use active, student-centered hands-on, approaches to creating interdependent communities in classrooms. *Developmentally Appropriate Practice in Early Childhood Programs* (Bredekamp and Copple, 1997) and *Yardsticks* (Wood, 1997) have also served as guides for Louise's practice.

Louise's Reflections

I built my practices on things I read about children and how they learn. I followed my state's curriculum closely in order to outline the academic goals for my students. I adapted and adopted from everything I read. I've been reading research summaries for years. I worked to incorporate these research findings into my classroom. I found developing my classroom based on these recommendations from research highly rewarding for my children and myself. I didn't spend one day in school bored or frustrated and the children learned and enjoyed learning.

Answering All the "Yes, Buts . . ."

Over the years, we have talked to many teachers in workshop presentations, in graduate classes, and individually. Louise's enthusiasm is infectious and teachers get interested in her classroom and her methods. Even after hearing her results and looking at the books she lends them, teachers worry and fret over doing things in unfamiliar ways. When we talk to teachers, they give us lots of "Yes, buts. . . ." They agree philosophically that children should be empowered and should take charge of their learning. They understand that "traditional methods" are often boring for the children and for teachers. But they hesitate. Their "yes, buts" come from their fear of changing and the possibilities of mistakes they may make if they try new things. The "yes, buts" become roadblocks that keep them from taking the journey to a child-centered classroom. Here are some of the roadblocks we have tried to help teachers remove.

How would you grade the children in this kind of classroom? How can you justify grades to parents?

Classroom grades—even letter or number grades—do not reflect any kind of absolute truth. Teacher evaluation that comes from outside the child may or may not be understood by the child. When evaluation is summative and used to produce a final grade or ranking, it usually does not lead to learning and improved work. A collection of artifacts for each child's portfolio provides both teacher, child, and parents with a clear picture of what the child can do and what he or she needs to work on. With input from children, teachers should develop guidelines or quality indicators based on the required curriculum. An emphasis on self-evaluation produces a higher quality of work from children by making them part of the evaluation process. Children should be asked, "What do you think you need to improve on?" Self-evaluation is based on children's understanding and creates self-improvement. Quality indicators thus help children self-evaluate and set goals.

Teachers and children can assess many different things besides right and wrong answers. For instance, other things that should be evaluated are participation and responsibility for materials and work. Children need to learn to get things in on time, to interact in positive, caring ways, do their work according to the quality indicators, work to the best of their abilities, and respond to feedback. Grades often don't assess progress in these areas. They generally rank children in relation to each other. Grades usually do not give valid information and are rarely true measures of understanding.

What you describe will take too much time. How can you spend so much time at the beginning of the year?

It does take time in the beginning. But there are big payoffs. As the year progresses, preparation takes less time inside and outside the classroom.

Louise's Reflections

Since I rarely used worksheets, I did *not* have to worry about finding them and running them off daily. The open-ended assignments I planned meant that the children created much of their own work. They had to do more writing and thinking than if I had used worksheets where they just filled in the blanks, colored, or drew lines. In their blank books they had to write their plans and record their work. They had to keep track of their reading and other work by filling out planners and reading logs. Later in the year, they kept up with special planning sheets for woodworking, cooking, and projects. They dated and filed their own work for their portfolios. Although Ella and I usually checked investigations and homework daily, I didn't have to check each child's work and recordings every day.

The children learned to take care of the room. They cleaned and helped prepare the room for the next day by being sure that materials were restocked and everything was in place. I couldn't take care of a room with as many materials and areas as this one by myself.

The children's work in their various books like investigations, reading logs, reflections books, and planners took over much of the intensive planning that many teachers need to do weekly and monthly. Instead of doing all the work herself and creating extensive thematic units for her children, Louise taught her children to create their own thematic projects.

Assessment was generally done with the children in school instead of by the teacher at home in isolation from the children. We conferenced weekly with each child and we did a lot of checking each day by walking around the room and "eyeballing" what the children were doing. Feedback was given directly to children while they were working or soon after any work was completed. Feedback was given during individual conferences and in group sharing of work.

Louise's Reflections

I did occasionally take a set of books home so that I could look at children's work over time. I enjoyed looking at their progress. I also had a list of the children's names on a chart so that I could make notes of things I wanted to remember to talk about with individual children or sometimes with the whole group.

Louise did not spend her day giving permission for things the children could manage themselves. The children learned to manage going to the bathroom, obtaining materials, sharpening pencils, and organizing their own work. The teacher didn't have to chastise and "shush" the children or yell because the children knew what to do and how to be respectful. Council meetings helped the children learn to solve many of their own problems so that the teacher was no longer the sole judge and jury. Cheating or copying other people's work were very rarely problems within this type of classroom structure.

Louise's Reflections

In March, April, and May, when other teachers complained of spring fever and kids who were weary and wild, my children were settled into an exciting routine and working hard. They were involved in projects of their own choosing. They did research with enthusiasm and taught their classmates what they had learned.

In a child-centered classroom, children want to come to school. Even on the last day of school, the children wanted to be there. Packing up at the end of school was a sad task for teachers and children because it signaled the impending loss of community.

I've been doing things the same way for many years. I can't start doing that because I don't know how.

How will you learn if you don't try? Nobody is born knowing everything that needs to be done in life or in a classroom. Learning to teach is developmental. No one leaves a teacher education program fully prepared for being a great teacher. Teaching well takes reflective practice over time. Risk taking is one key to change. Problem solving is another crucial element to successful program building. Next comes critiquing and reflection followed by more problem solving. All this leads gradually to improvement and growth.

Change and continuous improvement should be a way of life for teachers. Change comes gradually, one step at a time. Change often starts by reaching out for new insights. Teachers need to read books, professional journals, attend conferences and workshops, watch educational videos, and talk with other teachers. College courses at the master's level can bring experienced teachers exposure to new ideas and light the fires of change.

I am held accountable by the state. My kids have to take a standardized test.

Louise's children always had good test scores. Her methods and constant efforts to improve her practices paid off for her children. For years, when her children took standardized tests, they did very well. Recently, her second graders' writing abilities were tested and most scored *above* expected level on the test.

If you embrace a child-centered philosophy, believe in what you are doing, and teach well, your children's test scores will be fine. You must have faith in yourself, follow your curriculum guide, listen to what research says, and consider everything you know about children. Results speak for themselves.

The current emphasis on accountability through standardized testing has frightened many teachers. Some teachers believe that in order to prepare their children for the standardized tests, they must teach to those tests. They think they need to use drill and practice materials in the same formats as the tests. They are afraid to use methods and materials not directly related to what they assume will be tested. Day after day their children are subjected to drill and practice materials. We believe that practices such as teaching to the test and using test preparation materials all year will lead to bored, burnt out children and lower test scores.

The parents won't understand what I'm trying to do and won't like that kind of teaching.

Parent support is not automatic. Parents do need to be prepared for the differences. Letters and meetings at the beginning of the year are important. Parents need to know that the teacher has the curriculum and environment organized and that children will be held to high standards. Parent meetings and conferences at the beginning of the year and throughout the year are places to explain the changes in your program. Child-written newsletters, children's work, notes, phone calls, and student-led conferences keep parents informed. Over the years, Louise used a variety of interactive homework systems where children, their parents, and their teachers wrote back and forth to each other daily. The bottom line for most parents is a happy child who wants to go to school and the knowledge that their child is learning.

My administration won't let me do the things you suggest.

Parents can be a teacher's greatest advocate with the administration. Parents who appreciate teachers empower them. When children are happy, eager to go to school, and learning parents support their children's teachers. Parents who are happy with teachers do not complain to the principal or school board. Parents who are satisfied and supportive help teachers by giving administrators positive feedback. When a principal has many parents requesting that their children be in "Ms. Innovative Teacher's room" then they are likely to allow Ms. Innovative Teacher to continue improving her creative teaching strategies.

Change isn't easy and takes time and patience. Changing other people's minds can be difficult if not impossible. Sometimes just getting permission to try is enough. Most administrators want the best for their schools. Good administrators trust their teachers to know the curriculum and their children. We feel that the type of classroom we advocate produces both academic and social benefits for children. Administrators are impressed by results such as these.

Teachers who read professional materials can share them with administrators and colleagues. Professional groups like the National Association for the Education of Young Children, National Council of Teachers of Mathematics, National Council of Teachers of English, Whole Language Umbrella, Phi Delta Kappa, Association for Supervision and Curriculum Development, and Institute for Democracy in Education all can help support teachers in their quest for excellence and continuous improvement. When teachers cite research and practice to back up what they plan to do, then they are more likely to have credibility and permission.

Teachers should move beyond their school communities and do workshops and presentations at local, regional, and state conferences. Engaging colleagues in dialogue can be a powerful force for change. Support groups can help teachers advocate for quality and improvement.

I'm just plain scared that I can't handle it.

When teachers begin to work toward child-centered teaching, they worry about many things. Many teachers share fears that this type of classroom may be too noisy, too active, and perhaps out of control. They may worry that children may not be properly engaged in learning or on task. They may even be afraid that if they share power with their students, they will no longer be in control. These things can make people nervous, afraid to take risks, and afraid to make changes. We believe that these fears can be overcome with a mixture of faith, effort, persistence, and commitment to children.

We hope we have shown teachers how to establish a classroom community where power is shared, where children are active and interacting with each other, and where learning flows from children's innate curiosity and excitement. We believe that teachers can help children develop intrinsic motivation by tapping into their built-in desire to learn and grow. The challenge for teachers for the future is to provide an environment where children can express themselves well orally and in writing, and participate actively in their own learning. All this will lead to caring, capable, competent people of good character who will care for the world of tomorrow.

We hope that teachers will realize that the more power a teacher shares, the more influence that teacher will have. Powerful teachers who make a difference in children's lives do not force or try to dominate children. "You will do what I say or else" is counterproductive. Powerful teachers are in charge of their classes because they have earned the respect of the children and have created communities where children are empowered. A teacher with real power doesn't need to assert authority overtly because the children are cooperating as members of a close community. When problems arise, the teachers and children as members of the community work together to solve them. In a community, children can move around the room and interact with each other and their teachers in appropriate ways without chaos.

What Children Need

Effective teachers believe that children need time to observe, time to think, time to talk, and sometimes time to do things that might look to some people like "wasting time." In order to concentrate fully, people need to be able to alternate periods of relaxed activity with periods of intense concentration. Children must be allowed to have some control over their time and their environment. Teachers who believe that children need to be active, to experience, and to develop a love of learning must also allow children to make decisions about how they use their time. They must see that there are many routes to understanding. Effective teachers observe and listen to children so that they can hear and understand what their children are saying, thinking, and feeling (see Figure 5–1).

All Children Need to Be Empowered

Many people hearing about Louise's classroom would assume she was teaching very young children. All the traditional early childhood equipment is in place. However, we argue that most of the methods and materials in her room are suitable for all children in elementary school. Louise has used these methods and materials like sand, water, woodworking, cooking, and blocks successfully with children in fourth, fifth, and sixth grades. Although we realize that some materials and strategies would need to be modified for the upper grades, we believe that many things can remain the same. Many learning areas can be used by both primary and upper grades.

In the upper elementary grades when children have materials, opportunities, and choices, they can create more advanced work. Fine motor skills are better developed in older children. In order to provide for the many intelligences children come to school with, we need programs that provide them with many materials and experiences.

Louise's room was a rich storehouse of materials for discovery and learning. Much of the material was beautiful "junk" such as scraps of cloth, cardboard tubes, small boxes, lids, little rocks, buttons, and styrofoam shapes. Every year children from the upper grades who had been in Louise's class

In Mrs. Barrall's Room

By Cara

I enjoy learning because of the way Mrs. Barrall teaches. When we make mistakes she always says "Mistakes are just stepping stones to learning. Hope you improve next time! And she says it in sutch a kind and careing way. We have sutch a lot of centers. We don't do our work just at desks. We do it in centers. Every week we have a council meeting. We make dicions to help improve the room Mrs. barrall teaches us things we may need to know when we get bigger For example serving our-selves in the lunch-line and walking on the right-side of the hall. And that's what makes me exited about learning, Mr. Middleton I don't know about you, but of course, we're all different!!

Figure 5–1. *The classroom philosophy in a child's words.*

came to her room to gather supplies they needed for projects and plays they were working on in other classes.

If a teacher wants to promote active hands-on learning, then learning areas with a wealth of organized materials are a must. Many teachers worry that having learning areas may create more management problems. Actually, when children are taught how to use them, learning areas solve many problems. In the upper grades, having the materials organized, labeled, and available for easy access allows children to focus more on process and projects with less messing around and wasted time. Children in the upper grades are better able to do more detailed planning and reflections.

Challenges for the Future

We have a vision of a world where all people care for and respect each other and the earth. We want a world where people can work together to solve the daily problems we all face. We *choose* to believe that things can improve. We believe that the best hope for the future lies with our children and the people who teach them. If people are going to learn to live together and get along, they must be taught how to do these things. Schools can be part of the problem or part of the answer.

We believe that parents are their children's first teachers and are the most important people in their children's lives. We agree with the many people who feel that the primary responsibility for the development of children should lie with homes and parents. However, the world has changed and many needs that were once met primarily at home are no longer being adequately met. Families and communities are different. The tight-knit family and community structures that once existed have taken on new forms. Both parents are often working outside the home. Many families no longer live near extended families who could provide support.

Many people, including teachers, blame parents for things that go wrong in school. Some people resent the new demands made on schools to bridge gaps in children's lives. Again, we believe that blaming is counterproductive. While we know that parents retain primary responsibility for their children, we think schools must also take the responsibility of caring for children and for providing environments conducive to children's growth. We need to make changes where and when we can. To meet the needs of children in the new century, schools and teachers must be willing to accept new responsibilities.

Although some teachers still feel that the job of schools and teachers should be to teach facts and skills, we believe that this is not the whole picture. If we are to survive as a society, we have an obligation to go beyond facts and skills. We do not know today all that children will be required to know tomorrow. We must teach children how to access information and how to choose appropriate strategies in order to problem solve. This is an awesome task.

After more than thirty years in the classroom, Louise feels that she has only begun to explore the possibilities of working with children.

Louise's Reflections

My challenge to teachers is for them to continue this exploration by enhancing the education of children in ways that honor their individuality, and by helping them to be responsible, caring, lifelong learners. I see teaching as an evolving process.

As new approaches to teaching evolve and develop, educational paradigms will continue to shift. In this spirit we do not present this book as a how-to text. This is not a cookbook with step-by-step directions for creating a room just like Louise's. Good teaching evolves and changes each year as teachers and their children observe, reflect, and grow. We want to provide stepping stones for other teachers by sharing thoughts, showing possibilities, and providing illustrations of hard-learned lessons. Nobody needs to copy Louise day by day. Each teacher and each class of children are unique.

For teachers, the process of learning and growing is developmental just as it is for children. Teachers should have a vision of what they want their classrooms to be like and courage to take the risks necessary to transform their vision into reality. We hope this book helps these teachers move from vision to reality. We have tried to paint a clear picture of how to begin the year and create this special type of classroom. We have tried to describe the development of the class at the beginning of the year in enough detail so those teachers who share our vision can develop their own unique classroom communities. This book is for teachers like those who have visited Louise's room and left saying, "I want to teach like that. How does she do it?"

Modest Steps

Most teachers need to begin the change process with modest steps. Few are ready to plunge into the deep waters of student-centered education without fear of state mandates, standardized testing, and parental and administrator reactions. In most schools and in many teachers' minds, there is a very powerful "they" who won't let many teachers follow their hearts and explore new ways of teaching. We hope we have offered reassurance and suggestions for making the transition to teaching that embraces risk taking and change.

Observe Closely and Be Reflective

Teachers need to learn to observe children and systems closely every day and reflect on their classroom practices in order to be the best they can be. Risk takers must develop resiliency and learn to bounce back from experiences that do not bring immediate success. Great teachers do not settle for mediocrity. During the growth process, teachers need to learn to reach out to resources—media, print, and people who can help them find answers. They must trust their beliefs in children and learning. We firmly believe that teachers must be reflective, flexible, resilient, and risk takers. Great teachers continuously hone these habits of mind.

Professional Resources

This list is by no means comprehensive. But these are a few of our favorite books. We have left many more out.

Adler, M. 1984. *The Paideia Program—An Educational Syllabus.* New York: Macmillian Publishing Company.

Altwerger, B. and B. Flores. 1994. "Theme Cycles: Creating Communities of Learners," *Primary Voices K–6,* vol. 2, no. 1 (January): 2–13.

Apelman, M. and J. King. 1993. *Exploring Everyday Math Ideas for Students, Teachers, and Parents.* Portsmouth, NH: Heinemann.

Armington, D. 1997. *The Living Classroom—Writing, Reading, and Beyond.* Washington: National Association for the Education of Young Children.

Armstrond, T. 1994. *Multiple Intelligences in the Classroom.* Alexandria, VA: The Association for Supervision and Curriculum Development.

Ashton-Warner, S. 1963. *Teacher.* New York: Simon and Schuster.

Atwell, N. 1987. *In the Middle: Writing, Reading, and Learning with Adolescents.* Portsmouth, NH: Heinemann.

Avery, C. 1993. . . . *And with a Light Touch—Learning About Reading, Writing, and Teaching with First Graders.* Portsmouth, NH: Heinemann.

Bailey, B. 1996. *There's Gotta Be a Better Way: Discipline That Works!* Orlando, FL: Learning in Action.

Barker, J. 1993. *Paradigms. The Business of Discovering the Future.* New York: Harper Business.

Bateman, C. 1990. *Empowering Your Child: How to Help Your Child Succeed in School and in Life.* Norfolk, VA: Hampton Roads Publishing Company.

Bechtol, W. 1973. *Individualizing Instruction and Keeping Your Sanity.* Chicago: Follett Publishing.

Bellanca, J. 1992. *The Cooperative Think Tank II. Graphic Organizers to Teach Thinking in the Cooperative Classroom.* Palatine, IL: IRI/Skylight Publishing.

Bickart, T., J. Jablon, and D. T. Dodge. 1999. *Building the Primary Classroom: A Complete Guide to Teaching and Learning.* Portsmouth, NH: Heinemann.

Bickmore-Brand, J., ed. 1993. *Language in Mathematics.* Portsmouth, NH: Heinemann.

Black, H. and S. Black. 1990. *Organizing Thinking—Graphic Organizers.* Pacific Grove, CA: Midwest Publications.

Blackie, J. 1971. *Inside the Primary School.* New York: Shocken.

Bonstingl, J. 1992. *Schools of Quality. An Introduction to Total Quality Management in Education.* Alexandra, VA: Association for Supervision and Curriculum Development.

Bowan, T. and B. Bourne. 1994. *Thinking Like Mathematicians: Putting the K–4 NCTM Standards into Practice.* Portsmouth, NH: Heinemann.

Boyd, C. 1994. "Creating Curriculum for Children's Lives," *Primary Voices K–6,* vol. 2, no. 1 (January): 22–27.

Boyer, E. 1995. *The Basic School: A Community for Learning.* Princeton, NJ: Carnegie Foundation.

Bredekamp, S. and C. Copple, eds. 1997. *Developmentally Appropriate Practice in Early Childhood Programs.* Washington: National Association for the Education of Young Children.

Brooks, J. and M. Brooks. 1993. *In Search of Understanding: The Case for Constructivist Classrooms.* Alexandria, VA: The Association for Supervision and Curriculum Development.

Brown, J. 1995. *Observing Dimensions of Learning in Classrooms and Schools.* Alexandria, VA: The Association for Supervision and Curriculum Development.

Burke, K., R. Fogarty, and S. Belgrad. 1994. *The Mindful School: The Portfolio Connection.* Palatine, IL: IRI/Skylight Publishing.

Bybee, R., and J. McInerney, eds. 1995. *Redesigning the Science Curriculum.* Colorado Springs, CO: National Science Foundation.

Byham, W. 1992. *Zapp in Education: How Empowerment Can Improve the Quality of Instruction and Student and Teacher Satisfaction.* New York: Fawcett Columbine.

Byrnes, M. and R. Cornesky. 1994. *Quality Fusion: Turning Total Quality Management into Classroom Practice.* Port Orange, FL: Cornesky & Associates.

Byrnes, M., R. Cornesky, and L. Byrnes. 1993. *The Quality Teacher: Implementing Total Quality Management in the Classroom.* Bunnell, FL: Cornesky and Associates Press.

Calkins, L. 1994. *The Art of Teaching Writing.* Portsmouth, NH: Heinemann.

Cambourne, B. and J. Turbill. 1987. *Coping with Chaos.* Portsmouth, NH: Heinemann.

Campbell, L., B. Campbell, and D. Dickinson. 1996. *Teaching and Learning Through Multiple Intelligences.* Needham Heights, MA: Allyn & Bacon.

Chapman, C. 1993. *If the Shoe Fits . . . How to Develop Multiple Intelligences in the Classroom.* Palatine, IL: IRI/Skylight Publishing.

Charney, R. 1992. *Teaching Children to Care: Management in the Responsive Classroom.* Greenfield, MA: Northeast Foundation for Children.

Chuska, K. 1995. *Improving Classroom Questions.* Bloomington, IN: Phi Delta Kappa Educational Foundation.

Comer, J. 1993. "All Children Can Learn: A Developmental Approach," *Holistic Education Review,* vol. 6, no. 1 (Spring): 4–9.

Damon, W. 1988. *The Moral Child: Nurturing Children's Natural Moral Growth.* New York: The Free Press.

Daniels, H. 1994. *Literature Circles—Voice and Choice in the Student-Centered Classroom.* York, ME: Stenhouse Publishers.

Davies, A., C. Cameron, C. Politano, and K. Gregory. 1992. *Together Is Better: Collaborative Assessment, Evaluation, & Reporting.* Winnipeg, Canada: Peguis Publishers.

DeVries, R. and B. Zan. 1994. *Moral Classrooms, Moral Children: Creating a Constructivist Atmosphere in Early Education.* New York: Teachers College Press.

Dewey, J. 1916. *Democracy and Education.* New York: Free Press.

———. 1938. *Experience and Education.* New York: Macmillan Publishing Company.

Doris, E. 1991. *Doing What Scientists Do: Children Learn to Investigate Their World.* Portsmouth, NH: Heinemann.

Elkind, D. 1976. *Child Development and Education: A Piagetian Perspective.* New York: Oxford University Press.

Fogarty, R. 1995. *Best Practices for the Learner-Centered Classroom.* Palatine, IL: IRI/Skylight Publishing.

Gardner, H. 1993. *Multiple Intelligences: The Theory in Practice.* New York: Basic Books.

Gill, K. ed. 1993. *Process and Portfolios in Writing Instruction.* Urbana, IL: National Council of Teachers of English.

Glasser, W. 1998. *The Quality School.* New York: HarperCollins.

Glasser, W. and K. L. Dotson. 1998. *Choice Theory in the Classroom.* New York: Harper Perennial. Revised Edition.

Golub, J. 1994. *Activities for an Interactive Classroom.* Urbana, IL: National Council of Teachers of English.

Goodlad, J. 1990. *Teacher for Our Nation's Schools.* San Francisco, CA: Jossey-Bass Publishers.

Goodman, K. 1986. *What's Whole in Whole Language?* Portsmouth, NH: Heinemann.

Graves, D. 1983. *Writing: Teachers and Children at Work.* Portsmouth, NH: Heinemann.

————. 1989. *Experiment with Fiction.* Portsmouth, NH: Heinemann.

————. 1989. *Investigate Nonfiction.* Portsmouth, NH: Heinemann.

Hindley, J. 1996. *In the Company of Children.* York, ME: Stenhouse.

Holdaway, D. 1984. *Stability and Change in Literacy Learning.* Portsmouth, NH: Heinemann.

Hook, S. 1995. *John Dewey—An Intellectual Portrait.* Amherst, NY: Prometheus Books.

Hornsby, D., D. Sukarna, and J. Parry. 1986. *Read On: A Conference Approach to Reading.* Sydney, Australia: Martin Educational.

Hutton, D. 1994. *The Change Agents' Handbook: A Survival Guide for Quality Improvement Champions.* Milwaukee, WI: ASQC Quality Press.

Johnson, D., R. Johnson, and E. Holubec. 1994. *Cooperative Learning in the Classroom.* Alexandria, VA: The Association for Supervision and Curriculum Development.

Kamii, C. 1985. *Young Children Reinvent Arithmetic: Implications of Piaget's Theory.* New York: Teachers College Press.

Katz, L. G. and S. C. Chard. 1989. *Engaging Children's Minds: The Project Approach.* Norwood, NJ: Ablex.

Katz, L. G., and D. McClellan. 1997. *Fostering Children's Social Competence: The Teacher's Role.* Washington: National Association for the Education of Young Children.

Keefe, C. 1996. *Label-Free Learning: Supporting Learners with Disabilities.* York, ME: Stenhouse.

Kohn, A. 1993. *Punished by Rewards: The Trouble with Gold Stars, Incentive Plans, A's, Praise, and Other Bribes.* Boston: Houghton Mifflin.

————. 1996. *Beyond Discipline: From Compliance to Community.* Alexandria, VA: Association for Supervision and Curriculum Development.

Laminack, L. and K. Wood. 1996. *Spelling in Use: Looking Closely at Spelling in Whole Language Classrooms.* Urbana, IL: National Council of Teachers of English.

Lilburn, P. and P. Rawson. 1993. *Let's Talk Math: Encouraging Children to Explore Ideas.* Portsmouth, NH: Heinemann.

Marzano, R. 1992. *A Different Kind of Classroom: Teaching with Dimensions of Learning.* Alexandria VA: The Association for Supervision and Curriculum Development.

Marzano, R., R. Brandt, C. Huges, B. Jones, B. Presseisen, S. Rankin, and C. Suhor. 1988. *Dimensions of Thinking: A Framework for Curriculum and Instruction.*

McClanahan, E., and C. Wicks. 1993. *Future Force: Kids That Want To, Can, and Do!* Glendale, CA: Griffin Publishing.

Moline, S. 1995. *I See What You Mean.* York, ME: Stenhouse.

Montessori, M. 1967. *The Discovery of the Child.* New York: Ballantine Books.

Moon, J. and L. Schulman. 1995. *Finding the Connections: Linking Assessment, Instruction, and Curriculum in Elementary Mathematics.* Portsmouth, NH: Heinemann.

Neil, A. J. 1960. *Summerhill: A Radical Approach to Child Rearing.* New York: Hart.

Newkirk, T. and N. Atwell. 1988. *Understanding Writing.* Portsmouth, NH: Heinemann.

Norton, B. 1995. *The Quality Classroom Manager.* Amityville, NY: Baywood.

Nuffield Mathematics Project. 1975. *I Do, and I Understand.* New York: John Wiley.

Paley, V. 1981. *Wally's Stories.* Cambridge, MA: Harvard University Press.

Palmer, P. 1998. *The Courage to Teach: Exploring the Inner Landscape of a Teacher's Life.* San Francisco: Jossey-Bass Publishers.

Parry, J. and D. Hornsby. 1985. *Write On: A Conference Approach to Writing.* Portsmouth, NH: Heinemann.

Parsons, L. 1994. *Expanding Response Journals.* Portsmouth, NH: Heinemann.

Payne, J., ed. 1990. *Mathematics for the Young Child.* Reston, VA: National Council of Teachers of Mathematics.

Peterson, R. 1992. *Life in a Crowded Place: Making a Learning Community.* Portsmouth, NH: Heinemann.

Peterson, R. and M. Eeds. 1990. *Grand Conversations: Literature Groups in Action.* Richmond Hill, Ontario: Scholastic.

Pratt, C. 1970. *I Learn from Children.* New York: Harper & Row.

Purkey, W. and J. Novak. 1996. *Inviting School Success: A Self-Concept Approach to Teaching, Learning, and Democratic Practice.* Belmont, CA: Wadsworth.

Ray, K. W. 1999. *Wondrous Words: Writers and Writing in the Elementary Classroom.* Urbana, IL: National Council of Teachers of English.

Robinson, H. 1994. *The Ethnography of Empowerment: The Transformative Power of Classroom Interaction.* Washington: The Falmer Press.

Rogers, C. 1983. *Freedom To Learn for the 80s.* Columbus, OH: Merrill.

Rowe, G. 1991. *Guiding Young Artists Curriculum Ideas for Teachers.* Melbourne, Australia: Oxford University Press.

Schargel, F. 1994. *Transforming Education Through Total Quality Management: A Practitioner's Guide.* Princeton Junction, NJ: Eye on Education.

Schrenko, L. 1994. *Structuring a Learner-Centered School.* Palatine, IL: IRI / Skylight Publishing.

Sergiovanni, T. 1996. *Leadership for the Schoolhouse: How Is it Different? Why Is it Important?* San Francisco: Jossey-Bass.

Shipley, C. 1993. *Empowering Children—Play-Based Curriculum for Lifelong Learning.* Scarborough, Ontario: Nelson Canada.

Shockley, B., B. Michalove, and J. Allen. 1995. *Engaging Families Connecting Home and School Literacy Communities.* Portsmouth, NH: Heinemann.

Smith, F. 1997. *Reading Without Nonsense.* New York: Teachers College Press.

Sohns, M. and A. Buffington. 1977. *The Measurement Book.* Sunnyvale, CA: Enrich, Inc.

Soul, W., J. Reardon, A. Schmidt, C. Pearce, D. Blackwood, and M. D. Bird. 1993. *Science Workshop: A Whole Language Approach.* Portsmouth, NH: Heinemann.

Stauffer, R. 1970. *The Language-Experience Approach to the Teaching of Reading.* New York: Harper & Row.

Stearns, K. 1996. *School Reform—Lessons from England.* Princeton, NJ: The Carnegie Foundation.

Strickland, K. 1995. *Literacy, Not Labels: Celebrating Students' Strengths Through Whole Language.* Portsmouth, NH: Boynton/Cook Publishers.

Thompson, L. 1995. *Habits of the Mind—Critical Thinking in the Classroom.* Lanham, MD: University Press of America.

Wadsworth, B. 1978. *Piaget for the Classroom Teacher.* New York: Longman.

———. 1984. *Piaget's Theory of Cognitive and Affective Development.* New York: Longman.

Walker, L. 1982. *Carpentry for Children.* Woodstock, NY: The Overlook Press.

Wassermann, S. 1990. *Serious Players in the Primary Classroom—Empowering Children Through Active Learning Experiences.* New York: Teachers College Press.

Weber, L. 1971. *The English Infant School and Informal Education.* Engelwood Cliffs, NJ: Prentice-Hall.

Wilson, J. and L. Wing Jan. 1993. *Thinking for Themselves.* Portsmouth, NH: Heinemann.

Wood, C. 1997. *Yardsticks: Children in the Classroom Ages 4–14.* Greenfield, MA: Northeast Foundation for Children.

Zemelman, S., H. Daniels, and A. Hyde. 1998 2nd edition. *Best Practice: New Standards for Teaching and Learning in America's Schools.* Portsmouth, NH: Heinemann.

Favorite Children's Books
for the Beginning of the Year

Aesop's Fable. 1979. *The Town Mouse and the Country Mouse.* Mahwah, NJ: Troll Associates.

Berenstain, S. and J. Berenstain. 1982. *The Berenstain Bears Get in a Fight.* New York: Random House.

Burton, V. 1939. *Mike Mulligan and His Steam Shovel.* Boston, MA: Houghton.

Carle, E. 1983. *The Very Hungry Caterpillar.* New York: The Putman Publishing Company.

Carlson, N. 1958. *The Family Under the Bridge.* New York: Scholastic Book Services.

Cooney, B. 1982. *Miss Rumphius.* New York: Viking.

Cosgrove, S. 1983. *Gabby.* Los Angeles, CA: Price/Stern/Sloan.

———. 1985. *Squeakers.* Los Angeles, CA: Price/Stern/Sloan.

———. 1986. *Mumkin.* Los Angeles, CA: Price/Stern/Sloan.

———. 1987. *Buttermilk-Bear.* Los Angeles, CA: Price/Stern/Sloan.

———. 1987. *Memily.* Los Angeles, CA: Price/Stern/Sloan.

———. 1988. *Persnickity.* Los Angeles, CA: Price/Stern/Sloan.

———. 1988. *Rhubarb.* Los Angeles, CA: Price/Stern/Sloan.

———. 1988. *Sniffles.* Los Angeles, CA: Price/Stern/Sloan.

———. 1989. *The Grumpling.* Los Angeles, CA: Price/Stern/Sloan.

Fairfax, B. and A. Garcia. 1992. *Read! Write! Publish! Making Books in the Classroom.* Cypress, CA: Creative Teaching Press.

Flournoy, V. 1985. *The Patchwork Quilt.* New York: Dial.

Gramatky, H. 1939. *Little Toot.* New York: G. P. Putnam's Sons.

Harris, L., ed. 1954. *Aesop's Fables.* Garden City, NY: Doubleday and Company.

Hoban, L. 1964. *Bread and Jam for Frances.* New York: Harper and Row.

Hoffman, M. 1991. *Amazing Grace.* New York: Dial.

Laminack, L. 1998. *The Sunsets of Miss Olivia Wiggins.* Atlanta, GA: Peachtree.

Leaf, M. 1936. *The Story of Ferdinand.* UK: Puffin Publishing.

Peat, B. 1974. *The Wump World.* Boston, MA: Houghton Mifflin.

Piper, W. 1981. *The Little Engine That Could.* New York: Platt and Munk Publishers.

Schimmel, S. 1994. *Dear Children of the Earth.* Minocqua, WI: North Word Press.

Scholes, K. 1989. *Peace Begins with You.* San Francisco: Little, Brown and Company.

Sendak, M. 1962. *Pierre: A Cautionary Tale.* New York: HarperCollins.

———. 1963. *Where the Wild Things Are.* New York: Harper and Row.

Seuss, Dr. 1990. *Oh, The Places You'll Go!* New York: Random House.

Silverstein, S. 1964. *The Giving Tree.* New York: Harper and Row.

———. 1976. *The Missing Piece.* New York: HarperCollins.

———. 1981. *The Missing Piece Meets the Big O.* New York: HarperCollins.

Southgate, V. 1982. *The Enormous Turnip.* Lewiston, ME: Ladybird Books.

Steig, W. 1969. *Sylvester and the Magic Pebble.* New York: Simon and Schuster.

Tolstoy, L. 1968. *The Great Big, Enormous Turnip.* New York: Franklin Watts.

Zemach, M., ill. 1983. *The Little Red Hen: An Old Story.* New York: Farrar, Straus.